FTCE General Knowledge Exam

2nd Edition

By:
Kathleen Jasper, Ed.D.,
July 2018

NavaED
10600 Chevrolet Way #107
Estero, FL 33928

FTCE General Knowledge Exam
2nd Edition

Printed in the United States of America

ISBN-13: 978-1722029838

ISBN-10: 1722029838

The competencies in this book were designed and implemented by the Florida Department of
Education. Visit www.fl.nesinc.com for more information.

TABLE OF CONTENTS

GKT ENGLISH LANGUAGE SKILLS

GKT ENGLISH LANGUAGE SKILLS TEST SPECIFICATIONS

I. Knowledge of language structure

- Evaluate correct placement of modifiers.

- Apply knowledge of parallelism, including parallel expressions for parallel ideas.

- Apply knowledge of a variety of effective structures (e.g., recognizing fragments, comma splices, run-on sentences, syntax errors).

- Determine patterns of organization in a written passage (i.e., modes of rhetoric).

II. Knowledge of vocabulary application

- Determine the meaning of unknown words, multiple-meaning words, and phrases in context.

- Determine and select the correct use of commonly confused words, misused words, and phrases.

- Determine diction and tone appropriate to a given audience.

III. Knowledge of standard English conventions

- Determine and select standard verb forms.

- Determine and select inappropriate shifts in verb tense.

- Determine and select agreement between subject and verb.

- Determine and select agreement between pronoun and antecedent.

- Determine and select inappropriate pronoun shifts.

- Determine and select clear pronoun references.

- Determine and select pronoun case forms (e.g., subjective, objective, possessive).

- Evaluate the correct use of adjectives and adverbs.

- Determine and select appropriate comparative and superlative degree forms.

- Demonstrate command of standard spelling conventions.

- Demonstrate command of standard punctuation.

- Demonstrate command of standard capitalization.

KNOWLEDGE OF LANGUAGE STRUCTURE

1. Evaluate correct placement of modifiers.

2. Apply knowledge of parallelism, including parallel expressions for parallel ideas.

3. Apply knowledge of a variety of effective structures (i.e., recognizing fragments, comma splices, run-on sentences, syntax errors).

4. Determine patterns of organization in a written passage (i.e., modes of rhetoric).

MODIFIERS

A misplaced modifier is a word, phrase, or clause that is improperly separated from the word it modifies or describes. The separation causes an error that makes the sentence confusing.

Example:

> *Yolanda realized too late that it was a mistake to walk the neighbor's dog in high heels.*

The phrase *in high heels* modifies *the neighbor's dog* in this sentence. The dog is not in high heels; Yolanda is.

To correct the sentence, rearrange the sentence so the modifying clause is close to the word it should modify.

> *Yolanda realized too late that she shouldn't have worn high heels while walking the neighbor's dog.*

PARALLELISM

Parallelism refers to the same pattern of words or repetition of a chosen grammatical form within a sentence. Parallel structure is when a sentence follows the same grammatical pattern.

Example:

> *Pollution is caused by factories emitting smoke and cars spewing exhaust.*

> *Emitting* and *spewing* match in verb tense. They are parallel.

Non-example:

> *Pollution is caused by factories emitting smoke and cars that spew exhaust.*

> *Emitting* and *spew* do NOT match in verb tense. They are not parallel.

Example:

> *The business lost money because of inefficiency, theft and apathy.*

Non-example:

> *The business kept losing money because it was inefficient, the employees stealing money, and no one seemed to care.*

Example:

> *His strength, wit and advice were a comfort to me.*

Non-example:

> *His strength, wit and good advice were a comfort to me.*

EFFECTIVE STRUCTURES

COMMAS

Independent Clauses

Use commas to separate independent clauses when they are joined by any of these seven coordinating conjunctions: *and, but, for, or, nor, so, yet.*

Example:

> *I went to the store, and I bought a candy bar.*

Non-example:

> *I went to the store and I bought a candy bar.*

Unlike a semicolon, a comma alone *cannot* separate two independent clauses without a coordinating conjunction.

Example:

> *I went to the store, and I bought a candy bar.*

Non-example:

> *I went to the store, I bought a candy bar.*

Introductory Clauses

Use commas after introductory clauses, phrases, or words that come before the main clause.

Example:

> *After the movies, we went to get ice cream.*

Non-example:

> *Before we went out we got dressed up.*

SEMICOLONS

Use semicolons to separate two related independent clauses. Unlike commas, semicolons alone can separate two independent clauses. Semicolons do not need to be accompanied by a coordinating conjunction like *and, but, for, or, nor, so.*

Example:

> *I went to the store; I bought a candy bar.*

> *I love ice cream; chocolate is my favorite.*

Use semicolons between two independent clauses that are connected by conjunctive adverbs or transitional phrases.

Example:

> *I was excited to see my brother after so many years; surprisingly, he looked the same.*

KNOWLEDGE OF VOCABULARY APPLICATION

1. Determine the meaning of unknown words, multiple-meaning words, and phrases in context.
2. Determine and select the correct use of commonly confused words, misused words, and phrases.
3. Determine diction and tone appropriate to a given audience.

COMMONLY CONFUSED WORDS

Standardized English tests often include questions that include the following commonly confused words.

accept - to agree to receive or do
except - not including

adverse - unfavorable, harmful
averse - strongly disliking; opposed

advice - recommendations about what to do
advise - to recommend something

affect - to change or make a difference to
effect - a result; to bring about a result

aisle - a passage between rows of seats
isle - an island

all together - all in one place, all at once
altogether - completely; on the whole

along - moving or extending horizontally on
a long - referring to something of great length

aloud - out loud
allowed - permitted

altar - a sacred table in a church
alter - to change

amoral - not concerned with right or wrong
immoral - not following accepted moral standards

assent - agreement, approval
ascent - the action of rising or climbing up

bare - naked; to uncover
bear - to carry; to put up with

bated - in phrase *with bated breath*; in great suspense
baited - with bait attached or inserted

censure - to criticize strongly
censor - to ban parts of a book or film

cereal - a breakfast food
serial - happening in a series

coarse - rough
course - a direction; a school subject; part of a meal

complement - an addition that improves
compliment - to praise or express approval; an admiring remark

council - a group of people who manage or advise
counsel - advice; to advise

elicit - to draw out a reply or reaction
illicit - not allowed by law or rules

ensure - to make certain that something will happen
insure - to provide compensation

foreword - an introduction to a book
forward - onwards, ahead

principal - most important; the head of a school
principle - a fundamental rule or belief

sight - the ability to see
site - a location

stationary - not moving
stationery - writing materials

allusion - indirect reference
illusion - false idea

allude - to make indirect reference to
elude - to avoid

capital - major city, wealth, assets
capitol - government building

conscience - sense of morality
conscious - awake, aware

eminent - prominent, important
imminent - about to happen

everyday - routine, common
every day - each day, all the day

KNOWLEDGE OF STANDARD ENGLISH CONVENTIONS

1. Determine and select standard verb forms.

2. Determine and select inappropriate shifts in verb tense.

3. Determine and select agreement between subject and verb.

4. Determine and select agreement between pronoun and antecedent.

5. Determine and select inappropriate pronoun shifts.

6. Determine and select clear pronoun references.

7. Determine and select pronoun case forms (e.g., subjective, objective, possessive).

8. Evaluate the correct use of adjectives and adverbs.

9. Determine and select appropriate comparative and superlative degree forms.

10. Demonstrate command of standard spelling conventions.

11. Demonstrate command of standard punctuation.

12. Demonstrate command of standard capitalization.

SHIFTS IN VERB TENSE

A shift in verb tense is when the writer changes from one tense to another. Writers should avoid shifts in verb tense, especially while taking an English exam.

Example:

> Advocates of the school's meditation policy **believe** this practice helps prevent illness and stress; there **are** people who challenge this view.

These verb tenses match.

Non-example:

> Advocates of the school's meditation policy believe this practice **will help** prevent illness and stress. There **have been** people who challenged this view.

The verb tenses do not match.

SUBJECT-VERB AGREEMENT

The basic rule of subject-verb agreement is that a singular subject takes a singular verb, and plural subjects take a plural verb.

Example:

> <u>José goes</u> to the store after school.
> [singular]

> <u>José and his friends go</u> to the store after school.
> [plural]

Non-example:

> <u>José go</u> to the store after school.
> [singular]

> <u>José and his friends goes</u> to the store after school.
> [plural]

Subject-verb agreement gets more complicated when dealing with sentences that are more complex.

Example:

The use of cellphones and computers [is, are] prohibited.

The reader may think the subject of this sentence is plural because the words *cellphones* and *computers* are plural. However, *of cell phones and computers* is not the subject; it is the prepositional phrase that describes the type of use. *Use* is the subject of the sentence.

The use ~~of cellphones and computers~~ **is prohibited.**

DIRECTIONS: For questions 1–10, select the most appropriate word to complete the sentence.

1. Unfairly, the _____ of the cost has been paid by just a few members of the group.

    A. gift
    B. brunt
    C. choice
    D. divestiture

2. The committee seemed more concerned with long-term plans than with solving _____, immediate problems.

    A. apathetic
    B. ludicrous
    C. classic
    D. acute

3. Many ideas that used to be considered outrageous have become part of the _____.

    A. mainstream
    B. counterculture
    C. article
    D. gentry

4. The public was shocked when it became clear that Dr. Jackson's miraculous claims were in fact _____.

    A. inferior
    B. laughable
    C. bogus
    D. jealous

5. After war was declared, the army still needed a couple days to _____.

    A. mobilize
    B. reconstitute
    C. adjudicate
    D. remonstrate

6. It is _____ of her to assume she will get the job.

    A. pessimistic
    B. presumptuous
    C. cautious
    D. chaste

7. His flashy car, huge home, and expensive clothes _____ an air of snobbery.

    A. demurred
    B. concealed
    C. exuded
    D. abated

8. The teacher had trouble _____ her feelings of frustration when students misbehaved.

    A. maintaining
    B. distorting
    C. performing
    D. camouflaging

9. Pretending a problem doesn't exist won't help the situation; instead, it will only _____ it.

    A. exacerbate
    B. antagonize
    C. suppress
    D. exasperate

10. The technical terminology the professor used _____ his inexperienced students.

    A. amused
    B. deluded
    C. befuddled
    D. jaded

11. Without making a <u>sound Geoffrey crept</u> down the stairs.

    A. sound; Geoffrey crept
    B. sound, Geoffrey crept
    C. sound, crept Geoffrey
    D. No change is necessary.

12. At 15-years-old, he shipped as <u>a cabin boy, bound for</u> Ireland.

    A. a cabin boy; bound
    B. a cabin boy: bound for
    C. a cabin boy; bound for
    D. No change is necessary.

13. He knew he would get in trouble for skipping <u>school but he did it anyway.</u>

    A. school, he did it anyway.
    B. school and he did it anyway.
    C. school; he did it anyway.
    D. No change is necessary.

14. Gina had exams in the following <u>classes, math, history, and</u> science.

    A. classes; math, history, and
    B. classes: math, history, and
    C. classes, math, history, and
    D. No change is necessary.

15. Hector was <u>known as "Slim", because</u> of his gaunt appearance.

    A. known as "Slim," because
    B. known as "Slim." Because
    C. known as "Slim" because
    D. No change is necessary.

16. She <u>quickly sped up</u> to beat the red light.

    A. quickly
    B. sped up
    C. quick sped up
    D. No change is necessary.

17. The doctor's assistant mistakenly overbooked the schedule, <u>and causing frustration on the part of the doctor and the patients.</u>

    A. , causing frustration for the doctor and the patients.
    B. therefore causing frustration on the part of the doctor and the patients.
    C. and causing the effect of frustration for the doctor and the patients.
    D. No change is necessary.

18. When the flight attendant announced that no refreshments would be served on the flight,<u> each person</u> on board voiced their displeasure.

    A. all of the passengers
    B. each one
    C. every single person
    D. No change is necessary.

19. <u>Because she was not yet 18,</u> she could not purchase a Powerball ticket.

    A. The unfortunate consequence of her not being 18 was that
    B. Being that she was not 18 at the time,
    C. She was not 18 because
    D. No change is necessary.

20. <u>She forgot her list when she went to the grocery store;</u> this oversight caused her to forget many of the items she needed.

    A. Her list was forgotten at home when she went to the grocery store;
    B. Forgetting her list when she went to the grocery store,
    C. Because she forgot her list when she went to the grocery store,
    D. No change is necessary.

(1) The subject of whether or not Shakespeare should be studied in high school English classes has caused much debate. (2) On the one side, you have the diehard traditionalists who insist that learning to appreciate Shakespearean language is the crux of a well-rounded education. (3) However, others will argue that the archaic language used in Shakespeare's works is a source of confusion for students. (4) They also argue that today's students need more practice reading and interpreting the type of text they will be exposed to in a professional setting. (5) With valid arguments on both sides, this debate will most likely not be settled any time soon.

21. What is the best placement for the sentence below?

    They also point out that because many modern-day sayings have roots in his works, studying Shakespeare will help students grasp the history of our language.

    A. after sentence 4
    B. after sentence 2
    C. after sentence 5
    D. after sentence 1

(1) Many fear that with the onslaught of standardized testing, our students are not experiencing any joy in school, especially in the primary grades. (2) Seeing as though kids need to learn through play and discovery, there is good reason for concern. (3) Although teachers would love to encourage experiential learning by taking their students on field trips, there is little time in the schedule for such things. (4) Instead, children are stuck in front of a computer screen choosing multiple choice answers for complicated questions. (5) If we want to instill the joy of learning, we must allow more time for play and discovery.

22. What is the best re-write of sentence 2?

    A. Because research has proven that kids learn though play and discovery, this concern is valid.
    B. In light of the fact that kids learn through play and discovery, everyone should be concerned.
    C. Researchers know that children learn via play and discovery, so we should be concerned.
    D. It is a well-known fact that children need time to play and discover things, concern is warranted.

(1) For many beach communities, Spring Break means sold-out hotels, packed beaches, and crowded restaurants and bars. (2) While business owners love the crowds, many residents of these communities don't. (3) The extra traffic, lack of parking, and noisy partiers annoy those who just want to enjoy a peaceful day soaking up some sun and salt air. (4) However, their complaints usually fall on deaf ears as city officials allow Spring Breakers to take over. (5) It is unlikely that this issue will ever get resolved to everyone's satisfaction.

23. Which of the following is the best title for this piece?

    A. Spring Breakers Tell Residents to Take a Hike
    B. City Officials Refuse to Listen to Beach Residents
    C. Spring Break Crowds Cause Inconvenience to Residents
    D. Business Owners Vow to End the Spring Break Madness

(1) Many may think that manatees are only found in Florida. (2) However, Antillean manatees live in the coastal inland waterways of eastern Mexico, Central America, the Greater Antilles, and along the northern and eastern coasts of South America. (3) Florida manatees, although large in size, are docile and slow-moving creatures that will not harm people. (4) If you ever come across a Florida manatee in the water, there's no reason to be afraid, but remember to keep your hands to yourself.

24. What is the best placement for the sentence below?

Touching manatees can alter their behavior in the wild, causing them to lose their fear of boats and humans.

    A. Before sentence 1
    B. Before sentence 4
    C. Before sentence 2
    D. This sentence is not necessary

(1) You've probably heard the old adage, "no pain, no gain." (2) It is mostly associated with sports and physical training. (3) Most people wouldn't think this concept has anything to do with learning. (4) Just as you must push yourself physically to improve, you have to go beyond your limits mentally as part of the learning process. (5) After all, anything worth having is worthy of hard work.

25. Which is the best transition between sentences 3 and 4?

    A. Well, it does.
    B. Therefore, you can utilize this concept in learning applications.
    C. They are wrong.
    D. However, this idea can easily be applied to learning.

26. Choose the sentence that is grammatically correct:

    A. While she was out of town on business, a thief broke into her home, stealing her car, her computer, and taking her jewelry.
    B. While she was out of town on business, a thief had broken into her home, stole her car and computer, and took her jewelry.
    C. While out of town on business, a thief broke into her home, stole her car, computer, and her jewelry.
    D. While she was out of town on business, a thief broke into her home and stole her car, computer, and jewelry.

27. Choose the sentence that is grammatically correct:

    A. In danger of depleting their funds, the board of directors decided to settle the lawsuit rather than keep fighting.
    B. In danger of depleting its funds, the board of directors decided to settle the lawsuit in lieu of continuing to fight.
    C. Because their funds were being depleted, the board of directors decided to end the lawsuit by stopping the fight.
    D. The board of directions decided to settle the lawsuit instead of keep fighting since their funds were being depleted.

28. Choose the sentence that is grammatically correct.

    A. The teammates wore special uniforms in honor of their late coach.
    B. The teammates wore special uniforms in honor of its late coach.
    C. The teammates had worn special uniforms in honor of their late coach.
    D. The teammates have worn special uniforms in honor of its late coach.

29. Choose the sentence that is grammatically correct.

    A. A screw caused a pinging sound that was loose in the engine.
    B. The pinging sound caused by the loose screw in the engine.
    C. A loose screw was causing the pinging sound in the engine.
    D. A loose screw in the engine was causing the pinging sound.

30. Choose the sentence that is grammatically correct.

    A. She was the one that had the highest GPA in her class, so the girl was chosen to deliver the graduation speech.
    B. The girl with the highest GPA in the class was therefore chosen to deliver the graduation speech.
    C. Because she had the highest GPA in her class, the girl was chosen to deliver the graduation speech.
    D. Since she was chosen to deliver the graduation speech, the girl had the highest GPA in the class.

31. Choose the sentence that is grammatically correct.

    A.   Unaware of the bullying problem at her school, the principal was failing to respond appropriately.

    B.   Unaware of the bullying problem, the principal of the school had appropriately failed to respond.

    C.   Unaware of the bullying problem at her school, the principal failed to respond appropriately.

    D.   Unaware of the bullying problem, the principal failed to respond appropriately at her school.

32. Choose the sentence that is grammatically correct.

    A.   The fans at the back of the theater were making too much noise.

    B.   The fans at the back of the theater was making too much noise.

    C.   The fans at the back of the theater makes too much noise.

    D.   The fan at the back of the theater were making too much noise.

33. Choose the sentence that is grammatically correct.

    A.   Everyone on the crowded airplane were annoyed by the little girl running up and down the aisles.

    B.   Everyone crowded on the airplane were annoyed by the little girl running up and down the aisles.

    C.   Everyone on the crowded airplane was annoyed by the little girl running up and down the aisles.

    D.   Everyone crowded on the airplane were being annoyed by the little girl running up and down the aisles.

34. Choose the sentence that is grammatically correct.

    A.   Although I am not sure which, either my hard drive or one of my programs are not working properly.

    B.   Although I am not sure which, either my hard drive or one of my programs is not working properly.

    C.   Either, although I am not sure which, my hard drive or one of my programs is incorrectly working.

    D.   I am not sure which one it is, but either my hard drive or one of my programs are not working properly.

35. Choose the sentence that is grammatically correct.

    A.   The teacher asked the students, who were finished with their tests, to choose one of these options, read a book, write a story, or draw a picture.

    B.   The teacher asked the students, that were finished with their tests, to choose one of these options; read a book, write a story, or draw a picture.

    C.   The teacher asked the students, that were finished with their tests, to choose one of these options: read a book, write a story, or draw a picture.

    D.   The teacher asked the students, who were finished with their tests, to choose one of these options: read a book, write a story, or draw a picture.

Katherine is a volunteer basketball coach for the local YMCA. She needs to draft a letter that spells out the expectations for the participants and their parents.

36. Which would be the most professional closing line for Katherine's letter?

    A. I am looking forward to a great season and want to thank you in advance for your cooperation.

    B. This will be a great season if everyone cooperates and follows the guidelines set forth in this letter.

    C. I know that everyone thinks their child is special, but I believe that all of the children are special.

    D. I appreciate your cooperation and would also like to remind you that as a volunteer, I don't get paid.

Marco is a college student interested in the treasurer position for the local chapter of the Nursing Association at his school. He needs to send an email to the president of the association detailing why he believes he is a good candidate.

37. Which of the following best communicates his strengths?

    A. I am really into finances, am organized and detail-oriented, and will arrive to meetings on time.

    B. My strong math, organizational, and time-management skills make me a good candidate for the position.

    C. While good math skills are a plus, I believe that my ability to socialize is what the association needs.

    D. Being involved in extracurriculars looks good on a résumé, so I would like to take on this challenge.

Dr. Perez has decided to let an unreasonable, demanding patient go because of the way this man treats his staff members.

38. What would be the most diplomatic yet firm way to address this issue in a letter?

    A. Your demanding, demeaning and, quite frankly, immature behavior has left me no choice but to tell you to find another physician.

    B. I am not going to mince words: your behavior is unacceptable and cannot be tolerated in my practice, so you'll need to find another physician.

    C. I regret to inform you that I will no longer be able to serve as your physician and will send your records to your new physician upon request.

    D. At this time, I have to make the decision to let you go as a patient for fear of losing my staff, many of whom you have offended and abused.

Tina is interested in working as a teacher for an elite private school that rarely has openings. She wants to send her résumé so it is on file in the event a job does become available.

39. Which would be the most professional opening line for her cover letter?

    A. I understand that your institution rarely has openings, but I wanted to send you my impressive résumé just in case something does pop up.

    B. While I know you generally only hire people who know current employees, I thought it wouldn't hurt to send my résumé along.

    C. Please consider my extensive list of credentials as you conduct your end-of-year evaluations, as I may be a good replacement for someone.

    D. Although I understand that there are no current openings, I would like you to have my résumé on file in the event a position arises.

Ken has been unhappy with his lawn service for quite some time. He needs to give them a 30-day notice to end the contract.

40. Which would be the most positive way to end his letter?

    A. I appreciate your cooperation as we end our business relationship.

    B. If you give me a discount, I'll reconsider ending my contract.

    C. I plan on filing a complaint with the Better Business Bureau.

    D. I would never recommend you to anyone I know.

1.	B		24.	B
2.	D		25.	D
3.	A		26.	D
4.	C		27.	B
5.	A		28.	A
6.	B		29.	D
7.	C		30.	C
8.	D		31.	C
9.	A		32.	A
10.	C		33.	C
11.	B		34.	B
12.	D		35.	D
13.	C		36.	A
14.	B		37.	B
15.	C		38.	C
16.	B		39.	D
17.	A		40.	A
18.	A			
19.	D			
20.	D			
21.	B			
22.	A			
23.	C			

DIRECTIONS: For questions 1–10, select the most appropriate word to complete the sentence.

1. Unfairly, the _____ of the cost has been paid by just a few members of the group.

    A. gift - a present
    B. brunt - the burden
    C. choice - the option
    D. divestiture - the sale of business holdings

2. The committee seemed more concerned with long-term plans than with solving _____, immediate problems.

    A. apathetic - having little or no concern
    B. ludicrous - ridiculous
    C. classic - severing as a standard or model
    D. acute - intense, severe

3. Many ideas that used to be considered outrageous have become part of the _____.

    A. mainstream - trendy
    B. counterculture - rejecting trends or norms
    C. article - a piece of writing
    D. gentry - upper class

4. The public was shocked when it became clear that Dr. Jackson's miraculous claims were in fact _____.

    A. ersatz - synthetic, artificial
    B. laughable - funny, amusing
    C. bogus - not true
    D. jealous - resentment

5. After war was declared, the army still needed a couple of days to _____.

    A. mobilize - to assemble or marshal
    B. reconstitute - reconstruct
    C. adjudicate - to settle or determine
    D. remonstrate - to plea or protest

6. It is _____ of her to assume she will get the job.

    A. pessimistic - expecting bad things to happen
    B. presumptuous - bold, forward
    C. cautious - careful
    D. chaste - pure

7. His flashy car, huge home, and expensive clothes _____ an air of snobbery.

    A. demurred - objected
    B. concealed - covered up
    C. exuded - projected, displayed
    D. abated - reduced

8. The teacher had trouble _____ her feelings of frustration when students misbehaved.

    A. maintaining - keeping
    B. distorting - deforming
    C. performing - acting
    D. camouflaging - concealing

9. Pretending a problem doesn't exist won't help the situation; instead, it will only _____ it.

    A. exacerbate - increase the intensity of
    B. antagonize - to make hostile
    C. suppress - to do away with
    D. exasperate - to provoke

10. The technical terminology the professor used _____ his inexperienced students.

    A. amused - entertained
    B. deluded - misled
    C. befuddled - confused
    D. jaded - worn out

11. Without making a <u>sound Geoffrey crept</u> down the stairs.

    A. sound; Geoffrey crept
    B. sound, Geoffrey crept
       Introductory clauses should be followed by a comma. *Without making a sound* is an introductory clause.
    C. sound, crept Geoffrey
    D. No change is necessary.

12. At 15-years-old, he shipped as <u>a cabin boy, bound for</u> Ireland.

    A. a cabin boy; bound
    B. a cabin boy: bound for
    C. a cabin boy; bound for
    D. No change is necessary.
       A and C use the semicolon incorrectly. A semicolon is used when connecting two independent clauses, and *bound for Ireland* is not an independent clause. The colon in B is also used incorrectly. Therefore, a comma is the correct connector here, and no change is necessary.

13. He knew he would get in trouble for skipping <u>school but he did it anyway.</u>

    A. school, he did it anyway.
    B. school and he did it anyway.
    C. school; he did it anyway.
       The semicolon correctly separates the two independent clauses. A comma in answer A is not enough to separate two independent clauses. Just the *and* or the *but* is not enough to separate two independent clauses. A *comma and*, *comma but* is needed.
    D. No change is necessary.

14. Gina had exams in the following <u>classes, math, history, and</u> science.

    A. classes; math, history, and
    B. classes: math, history, and
       The colon used when an independent clause (*Gina had exams in the following classes*) is followed by a list. (*math, history, and science*).
    C. classes, math, history, and
    D. No change is necessary.

15. Hector was known as "Slim", because of his gaunt appearance.

    A. known as "Slim," because
    B. known as "Slim." Because
    C. known as "Slim" because
       No comma is needed before *because*.
    D. No change is necessary.

16. She <u>quickly sped up</u> to beat the red light.

    A. quickly

    B. sped up

    Sped up* means quickly, so quickly is not necessary. It is redundant. Leave out *quickly* and use only *sped up.

    C. quick sped up

    D. No change is necessary.

17. The doctor's assistant mistakenly overbooked the schedule<u>, and causing frustration on the part of the doctor and the patients.</u>

    A. , causing frustration for the doctor and the patients.

    The dependent clause must be preceded by a comma. *Comma and* is the necessary conjunction when two independent clauses are linked.

    B. therefore causing frustration on the part of the doctor and the patients.

    C. and causing the effect of frustration for the doctor and the patients.

    D. No change is necessary.

18. When the flight attendant announced that no refreshments would be served on the flight,<u> each person</u> on board voiced their displeasure.

    A. all of the passengers

    This is pronoun/antecedent agreement. Switch *each person* to *all of the passengers* so *their* matches the subject.

    B. each one

    C. every single person

    D. No change is necessary.

19. <u>Because she was not yet 18,</u> she could not purchase a Powerball ticket.

    A. The unfortunate consequence of her not being 18 was that

    B. Being that she was not 18 at the time,

    C. She was not 18 because

    D. No change is necessary.

    You can start a sentence with *Because* when it is an introductory clause. As you can see, in the sentence above, *Because she was not yet eighteen*, is an introductory clause followed by a complete sentence, *she could not purchase a Powerball ticket*. Therefore, no change is necessary.

20. <u>She forgot her list when she went to the grocery store;</u> this oversight caused her to forget many of the items she needed.

    A. Her list was forgotten at home when she went to the grocery store;

    B. Forgetting her list when she went to the grocery store,

    C. Because she forgot her list when she went to the grocery store,

    D. No change is necessary.

    The semicolon is used correctly in this sentence. It connects two related independent clauses. Therefore, no change is necessary.

21. *(1) The subject of whether or not Shakespeare should be studied in high school English classes has caused much debate. (2) On the one side, you have the diehard traditionalists who insist that learning to appreciate Shakespearean language is the crux of a well-rounded education. (3) However, others will argue that the archaic language used in Shakespeare's works is a source of confusion for students. (4) They also argue that today's students need more practice reading and interpreting the type of text they will be exposed to in a professional setting. (5) With valid arguments on both sides, this debate will most likely not be settled any time soon.*

What is the best placement for the sentence below?

They also point out that because many modern-day sayings have roots in his works, studying Shakespeare will help students grasp the history of our language.

    A. after sentence 4

    B. after sentence 2

    The best placement of the above sentence is after this sentence because sentence 2 talks about Shakespearean language.

    C. after sentence 5

    D. after sentence 1

22. *(1) Many fear that with the onslaught of standardized testing, our students are not experiencing any joy in school, especially in the primary grades. (2) Seeing as though kids need to learn through play and discovery, there is good reason for concern. (3) Although teachers would love to encourage experiential learning by taking their students on field trips, there is little time in the schedule for such things. (4) Instead, children are stuck in front of a computer screen choosing multiple-choice answers for complicated questions. (5) If we want to instill the joy of learning, we must allow more time for play and discovery.*

What is the best re-write of sentence 2?

    A. Because research has proven that kids learn though play and discovery, this concern is valid.

    You can start a sentence with *Because* when it is an introductory clause. In this case, this sentence is grammatically and stylistically correct.

    B. In light of the fact that kids learn through play and discovery, everyone should be concerned.

    C. Researchers know that children learn via play and discovery, so we should be concerned.

    D. It is a well-known fact that children need time to play and discover things, concern is warranted.

23. *(1) For many beach communities, Spring Break means sold-out hotels, packed beaches, and crowded restaurants and bars. (2) While business owners love the crowds, many residents of these communities don't. (3) The extra traffic, lack of parking, and noisy partiers annoy those who just want to enjoy a peaceful day soaking up some sun and salt air. (4) However, their complaints usually fall on deaf ears as city officials allow Spring Breakers to take over. (5) It is unlikely that this issue will ever get resolved to everyone's satisfaction.*

Which of the following is the best title for this piece?

    A. Spring Breakers Tell Residents to Take a Hike

    B. City Officials Refuse to Listen to Beach Residents

    C. <u>Spring Break Crowds Cause Inconvenience to Residents</u>

        This title includes all the main ideas discussed in the passage.

    D. Business Owners Vow to End the Spring Break Madness

24. *(1) Many may think that manatees are only found in Florida. (2) However, Antillean manatees live in the coastal inland waterways of eastern Mexico, Central America, the Greater Antilles, and along the northern and eastern coasts of South America. (3) Florida manatees, although large in size, are docile and slow-moving creatures that will not harm people. (4) If you ever come across a Florida manatee in the water, there's no reason to be afraid, but remember to keep your hands to yourself.*

What is the best placement for the sentence below?

Touching manatees can alter their behavior in the wild, causing them to lose their fear of boats and humans.

    A. Before sentence 1

    B. <u>Before sentence 4</u>

        This sentence is an effective transition to the last cautionary sentence.

    C. Before sentence 2

    D. This sentence is not necessary

25. *(1) You've probably heard the old adage, "no pain, no gain." (2) It is mostly associated with sports and physical training. (3) Most people wouldn't think this concept has anything to do with learning. (4) Just as you must push yourself physically to improve, you have to go beyond your limits mentally as part of the learning process. (5) After all, anything worth having is worthy of hard work.*

Which is the best transition between sentences 3 and 4?

    A. Well, it does.

    B. Therefore, you can utilize this concept in learning applications.

    C. They are wrong.

    D. <u>However, this idea can easily be applied to learning.</u>

        This sentence is the best transition because it gives an alternative to sentence 3.

26. Choose the sentence that is grammatically correct.

    A. While she was out of town on business, a thief broke into her home, stealing her car, her computer, and taking her jewelry.
    B. While she was out of town on business, a thief had broken into her home, stole her car and computer, and took her jewelry.
    C. While out of town on business, a thief broke into her home, stole her car, computer and her jewelry.
    D. **While she was out of town on business, a thief broke into her home and stole her car, computer and jewelry.**
       This list is parallel. The other answer choices are not parallel.

27. Choose the sentence that is grammatically correct.

    A. In danger of depleting their funds, the board of directors decided to settle the lawsuit rather than keep fighting.
    B. **In danger of depleting its funds, the board of directors decided to settle the lawsuit in lieu of continuing to fight.**
       Though it is composed of a group of people, the *board of directors* is a collective noun that refers to a singular entity. Therefore, *its* is correct because it is a singular possessive pronoun. *Their* is incorrect because it is a plural possessive pronoun.
    C. Because their funds were being depleted, the board of directors decided to end the lawsuit by stopping the fight.
    D. The board of directions decided to settle the lawsuit instead of keep fighting since their funds were being depleted.

28. Choose the sentence that is grammatically correct.

    A. **The teammates wore special uniforms in honor of their late coach.**
       Teammates is plural, so *their* is correct because it is a plural possessive pronoun.
    B. The teammates wore special uniforms in honor of its late coach.
    C. The teammates had worn special uniforms in honor of their late coach.
    D. The teammates have worn special uniforms in honor of its late coach.

29. Choose the sentence that is grammatically correct.

    A. A screw caused a pinging sound that was loose in the engine.
    B. The pinging sound caused by the loose screw in the engine.
    C. A pinging screw was causing the engine.
    D. **A loose screw in the engine was causing the pinging sound.**
       This sentence has the correctly placed modifier.

30. Choose the sentence that is grammatically correct.

    A. She was the one that had the highest GPA in her class, so the girl was chosen to deliver the graduation speech.

    B. The girl with the highest GPA in the class was therefore chosen to deliver the graduation speech.

    C. <u>Because she had the highest GPA in her class, the girl was chosen to deliver the graduation speech.</u>

    Use a comma to link a dependent introductory clause to an independent clause. If the sentence were flipped, no comma would be needed.

    D. Since she was chosen to deliver the graduation speech, the girl had the highest GPA in the class.

31. Choose the sentence that is grammatically correct.

    A. Unaware of the bullying problem at her school, the principal was failing to respond appropriately.

    B. Unaware of the bullying problem, the principal of the school had appropriately failed to respond.

    C. <u>Unaware of the bullying problem at her school, the principal failed to respond appropriately.</u>

    Correct comma use and tense agreement.

    D. Unaware of the bullying problem, the principal failed to respond appropriately at her school.

32. Choose the sentence that is grammatically correct.

    A. <u>The fans at the back of the theater were making too much noise.</u>

    Subject-verb agreement. The *fans were making too much noise*.

    B. The fans at the back of the theater was making too much noise.

    C. The fans at the back of the theater makes too much noise.

    D. The fan at the back of the theater were making too much noise.

33. Choose the sentence that is grammatically correct.

    A. Everyone on the crowded airplane were annoyed by the little girl running up and down the aisle.

    B. Everyone crowded on the airplane were annoyed by the little girl running up and down the aisle.

    C. <u>Everyone on the crowded airplane was annoyed by the little girl running up and down the aisle.</u>

    Subject-verb agreement. *Everyone was annoyed*.

    D. Everyone crowded on the airplane were being annoyed by the little girl running up and down the aisle.

34. Choose the sentence that is grammatically correct.

   A. Although I am not sure which, either my hard drive or one of my programs are not working properly.

   B. <u>Although I am not sure which, either my hard drive or one of my programs is not working properly.</u>

      Subject-verb agreement. *My hard drive is not working. One of my programs is not working. One* **is singular.**

   C. Either, although I am not sure which, my hard drive or one of my programs is incorrectly working.

   D. I am not sure which one it is, but either my hard drive or one of my programs are not working properly.

35. Choose the sentence that is grammatically correct.

   A. The teacher asked the students, who were finished with their tests, to choose one of these options, read a book, write a story, or draw a picture.

   B. The teacher asked the students, that were finished with their tests, to choose one of these options; read a book, write a story, or draw a picture.

   C. The teacher asked the students, that were finished with their tests, to choose one of these options: read a book, write a story, or draw a picture.

   D. <u>The teacher asked the students, who were finished with their tests, to choose one of these options: read a book, write a story, or draw a picture.</u>

      Colons are used to connect an independent clause with a list.

Katherine is a volunteer basketball coach for the local YMCA. She needs to draft a letter that spells out the expectations for the participants and their parents.

36. Which would be the most appropriate closing line for Katherine's letter?

   A. **I am looking forward to a great season and want to thank you in advance for your cooperation.**
   This is most appropriate. It is positive and helpful.
   B. This will be a great season if everyone cooperates and follows the guidelines set forth in this letter.
   C. I know that everyone thinks their child is special, but I believe that all of the children are special.
   D. I appreciate your cooperation and would also like to remind you that as a volunteer, I don't get paid.

Marco is a college student interested in the treasurer position for the local chapter of the Nursing Association at his school. He needs to send an email to the president of the association detailing why he believes he is a good candidate.

37. Which of the following best communicates his strengths?

   A. I am really into finances, am organized and detail-oriented, and will arrive to meetings on time.
   B. **My strong math, organizational, and time-management skills make me a good candidate for the position.**
   This sentence provides strong, concise reasons why he should be considered for the job and is written in a professional manner.
   C. While good math skills are a plus, I believe that my ability to socialize is what the association needs.
   D. Being involved in extracurriculars looks good on a résumé, so I would like to take on this challenge.

Dr. Perez has decided to let an unreasonable, demanding patient go because of the way this man treats his staff members.

38. What would be the most diplomatic yet firm way to address this issue in a letter?

   A. Your demanding, demeaning and, quite frankly, immature behavior has left me no choice but to tell you to find another physician.
   B. I am not going to mince words: your behavior is unacceptable and cannot be tolerated in my practice, so you'll need to find another physician.
   C. **I regret to inform you that I will no longer be able to serve as your physician and will send your records to your new physician upon request.**
   This sentence is direct and professional.
   D. At this time, I have to make the decision to let you go as a patient for fear of losing my staff, many of whom you have offended and abused.

Tina is interested in working as a teacher for an elite private school that rarely has openings. She wants to send her résumé so it is on file in the event a job does become available.

39. Which would be the most professional opening line for her cover letter?

A. I understand that your institution rarely has openings, but I wanted to send you my impressive résumé just in case something does pop up.

B. While I know you generally only hire people who know current employees, I thought it wouldn't hurt to send my résumé along.

C. Please consider my extensive list of credentials as you conduct your end-of-year evaluations as I may be a good replacement for someone.

D. **Although I understand that there are no current openings, I would like you to have my résumé on file in the event a position arises.**
This sentence is direct and professional.

Ken has been unhappy with his lawn service for quite some time. He needs to give them a 30- day notice to end the contract.

40. Which would be the most professional way to end his letter?

A. **I appreciate your cooperation as we end our business relationship.**
This sentence is professional and straightforward.

B. If you give me a discount, I'll reconsider ending my contract.

C. I plan on filing a complaint with the Better Business Bureau.

D. I would never recommend you to anyone I know.

DIRECTIONS: For questions 1–10, select the most appropriate word to complete the sentence.

1. Much to his _____, the student did not get accepted into the college of his choice.

   A. revelry
   B. chagrin
   C. confidence
   D. disdain

2. We felt empathy for the disheveled, _____ homeless man begging for money.

   A. tidy
   B. unkempt
   C. orderly
   D. immaculate

3. During freshman orientation, the students were feverishly taking _____ notes.

   A. copious
   B. verbose
   C. loquacious
   D. scant

4. The teacher _____ the class for its _____ behavior on the field trip.

   A. chastised, unruly
   B. commended, unruly
   C. chastised, orderly
   D. reprimanded, orderly

5. As she prepared to move into the dorm, it dawned on her that she had _____ too many things.

   A. accounted
   B. accredited
   C. accumulated
   D. accrued

6. The _____ professor refused to grade any assignments that did not follow his exact instructions.

   A. pompous
   B. scrupulous
   C. cautious
   D. fastidious

7. _____ is not a good quality in a physician.

    A. resolution
    B. arrogance
    C. fortitude
    D. empathy

8. When the ambulance arrived, the _____ patient refused to cooperate.

    A. complacent
    B. submissive
    C. indelible
    D. obstinate

9. In a world of conflict, she attempted to be _____.

    A. contentious
    B. sanguine
    C. conducive
    D. intolerant

10. After much debate, the council members could not reach a _____ at the meeting, forcing them to table the decision.

    A. consensus
    B. conclusion
    C. cessation
    D. concurrence

11. Her list of complaints about the apartment was long; bad view, too noisy, ugly carpet, and small kitchen.

    A. long, bad view,
    B. long (bad view,)
    C. long: bad view,
    D. No change is necessary.

12. Now that he was 18, he thought he didn't need his parents.

    A. Now that he was 18
    B. Now that he was 18;
    C. Now that he was 18:
    D. No change is necessary.

13. Stop! Shouted the frustrated mother.

    A. "Stop!" shouted
    B. "Stop!", shouted
    C. "Stop!" Shouted
    D. No change is necessary.

14. The advisor gave Tim a list of the courses he needed for his program: Macro Economics, Business Law, and Financial Accounting.

    A. Program - Macro Economics, Business Law, and Financial Accounting.
    B. program: macro economics, business law, and financial accounting.
    C. program. Macro Economics, Business Law, and Financial Accounting.
    D. No change is necessary.

15. When he found out he failed the test yet again he decided college was not for him.

    A. yet again; he decided
    B. yet, again, he decided
    C. yet again, he decided
    D. No change is necessary.

16. The tiny diminutive girl was not tall enough for the rollercoaster.

    A. tiny, diminutive
    B. diminutive
    C. diminutive,
    D. No change is necessary.

17. <u>Unfortunately she forgot</u> the most important part of the birthday celebration: the gift.

  - A. She, unfortunately forgot
  - B. She unfortunately, forgot
  - C. Unfortunately, she forgot
  - D. No change is necessary.

18. When the state officials announced huge budget cuts in <u>education administrators, teachers, and parents</u> were livid.

  - A. education, administrators, teachers, and parents
  - B. education, administrators teachers and parents
  - C. education, administrators and teachers, parents
  - D. No change is necessary.

19. His feelings were hurt <u>when the chocolates he gave the girl were rejected.</u>

  - A. when the girl rejected the chocolates which he gave her.
  - B. when the girl rejected the chocolates that he gave her.
  - C. when the girl rejected the chocolates, that he gave her.
  - D. No change is necessary.

20. The CFO warned his staff <u>not to talk at the media</u> about the incident.

  - A. not to talk for the media
  - B. to not speak to the media
  - C. not to speak to the media
  - D. No change is necessary.

21. Determine the purpose of the parentheses.

    Marisa (who was busy texting her friend) ignored her mother's request to empty the dishwasher.

    A. to clarify who ignored the mother's request
    B. to introduce a new person into the situation
    C. to enclose information that clarifies the situation
    D. to add humor to the tense situation

22. Determine the purpose of the apostrophe.

    The child's favorite toy was misplaced.

    A. to replace the *i* in the word is to form a contraction
    B. to indicate that the toy belonged to the child
    C. to make the word child plural
    D. to show that more than one child owned the toy

23. Determine the purpose of the parentheses.

    The teammates (accompanied by their coach) had a celebratory dinner after their victory.

    A. to include the coach as part of the subject
    B. to show that the coach was an afterthought
    C. to clarify that the coach also attended the dinner
    D. to diminish the role that the coach played

24. Choose the sentence in which the apostrophe is accurately placed.

    A. The boys decided it would be funny to steal the girls' books as payback for telling the teacher they cheated on the last test.
    B. The boys' decided it would be funny to steal the girls books as payback for telling the teacher they cheated on the last test.
    C. The boys decided it would be funny to steal the girls's books as payback for telling the teacher they cheated on the last test.
    D. The boy's decided it would be funny to steal the girls books as payback for telling the teacher they cheated on the last test.

25. Choose the sentence in which the parentheses are accurately placed.

    A. Joey and (his mother) continued to drive well after he realized they were lost.
    B. Joey and his mother continued (to drive) well after he realized they were lost.
    C. Joey and his mother (continued to) drive well after he realized they were lost.
    D. Joey (and his mother) continued to drive well after he realized he was lost.

(1) "What do you want to be when you grow up?" (2) It's a question that adults commonly ask school-aged children. (3) Some of the traditional answers include: doctor, nurse, firefighter, teacher, and police officer. (4) However, students today may have their sights set on more a more technical career such as social media architect, data scientist, computer software engineer, or network systems analyst. (5) And, as technology continues to race forward at lightning speed, new job titles will be created to support consumer demand. (6) The simple question, "What do you want to be when you grow up?" may have some answers that have adults scratching their heads.

26. What is the best placement for the sentence below?

    Many of these careers are familiar to kids who have grown up with technology but not so familiar to many adults.

    A. before sentence 6
    B. after sentence 3
    C. after sentence 4
    D. before sentence 3

(1) Many worry that children are getting too much screen time. (2) In the past, television was about the only screen parents needed to monitor. (3) However, with technology, children are exposed to screens not only through television but also through phones, tablets, in-car entertainment centers, and computers. (4) How much is too much? (5) Not everyone agrees, but many experts say children under 2 should have no screen time, and children over 2 should have no more than 2 hours per day of screen time.

27. Which would be the best concluding sentence after sentence 5?

    A. Whether or not you agree with these strict guidelines, you should always do what the experts suggest.
    B. Although these recommendations are unrealistic, you should consider them when deciding on how much screen time to give a child.
    C. If you want to be a good parent, you need to follow these expert recommendations regardless of how unrealistic they may seem.
    D. While many would argue these guidelines are not realistic, they do bring attention to the need to monitor and limit a child's daily screen time.

(1) Many retirees chose to spend their golden years in warmer climates. (2) Florida and California have been popular options for these folks. (3) However, arid Arizona has grown as a favorite place to retire. (4) In addition, Arizona generally avoids natural disasters and never gets hit with hurricanes or earthquakes. (5) Beyond the sunny, warm, and dry climate, Arizona is also an affordable place to live. (6) No wonder it has become a retirement destination for many.

28. Which of the following is the best title for this passage?

    A. Arizona Attracts More and More Retirees
    B. Arizona Beating Out Florida as a Retirement Destination
    C. Arizona Heat Too Much for the Aging Population
    D. Arizona Faces the Heat as a Retirement Community

(1) There is a national crisis looming, one that has the potential to affect millions of American children. (2) While this assessment may sound dramatic, the national teacher shortage already affects students across our country. (3) But, many current teachers will attest that increasing workloads, unrealistic expectations, and low salaries are to blame for veteran teachers calling it quits. (4) Students are packed into classrooms when schools do not have enough teachers to keep class sizes low, and in worst case scenarios, kids are held in auditoriums or gyms when there are no teachers at all. (5) Unfortunately, there is no single factor causing this. (6) Decreasing the work load and increasing pay would certainly go a long way to retaining current teachers and attracting new ones.

29. What is the best sentence order to provide a logical sequence of ideas?

      A. 6, 1, 2, 3, 4, 5
      B. 1, 2, 4, 5, 3, 6
      C. 1, 3, 2, 5, 4, 6
      D. 6, 5, 2, 3, 1, 4

(1) All over America, vending machines at schools have been emptied of any drinks with sugar. (2) Those sweet and calorie-laden cans of soda, sports drinks, and flavored water were replaced with "diet" versions, purportedly because they are healthier options. (3) However, how healthy is it for kids to consume these artificial sweeteners on a daily basis? (4) Over the years, research has shown that sugar substitutes can increase sugar cravings. (5) All of this raises an important question: Have the changes to vending machine offerings made kids healthier or just replaced one unhealthy option with another?

30. Which sentence would fit best between sentences 4 and 5?

      A. This, unfortunately, will just cause obesity rates to rise among our children.
      B. Research has also linked daily use of these products to certain health issues.
      C. However, nutritional guidelines are always changing, so who knows.
      D. So, kids who drink diet sodas are less likely to exercise and thus gain weight.

31. Choose the sentence that is grammatically correct.

    A. Many will agree that public servants such as nurses, firefighters, police officers, social workers, and teachers need to be paid better salaries.
    B. Many will agree that public servants: such as nurses; firefighters; police officers; social workers; and teachers need to be paid better salaries.
    C. Many will agree that public servants such as: nurses, firefighters, police officers, social workers, and teachers need to be paid better salaries.
    D. Many will agree that public servants such as nurses, firefighters and police officers, social workers and teachers need to be paid better salaries.

32. Choose the sentence that is grammatically correct.

    A. Cyber-bullying has become an issue, with the spike in social media use.
    B. Cyber-bullying has become an issue, because of the spike in social media use.
    C. Cyber-bullying has become an issue; with the spike in social media use.
    D. With the spike in social media use, cyber-bullying has become an issue.

33. Choose the sentence that is grammatically correct.

    A. The patients in the medical trial received compensation for they're participation.
    B. The patients in the medical trial received compensation for there participation.
    C. The patients in the medical trial received compensation for their participation.
    D. The patients in the medical trial received compensation for his or her participation.

34. Choose the sentence that is grammatically correct.

    A. With fuel prices plummeting, many are perplexed by the increase of airline ticket prices.
    B. With fuel prices plummeting, the price increase in airline tickets is perplexing.
    C. With the price of fuel plummeting, increases in airline tickets perplexes.
    D. With the price of fuel plummeting, increased airline tickets remains perplexed.

35. Choose the sentence that is grammatically correct.

    A. He was the only one in the class who read the assigned chapters.
    B. He was the only one in the class that read the assigned chapters.
    C. He was the only one in the class which read the assigned chapters.
    D. He was the only one in the class whom read the assigned chapters.

36. Choose the sentence that communicates an idea clearly.

    A. As each hour passed, the mother's concern increased that her son wasn't home yet.
    B. With each passing hour, the mother became concerned increasingly that her son wasn't home yet.
    C. As each hour passed by, the concern of the mother increased that her son wasn't home yet.
    D. With each passing hour, the mother became increasingly concerned that her son wasn't home yet.

37. Choose the sentence that is grammatically correct.

    A. The use of cell phones and computers have been prohibited.
    B. The use of cell phones and computers were prohibited.
    C. The use of cell phones and computers is prohibited.
    D. The use of cell phones and computers are prohibited.

38. Choose the sentence that is grammatically correct.

    A. Everyone on the crowded subway were flustered when the train screeched to a halt.
    B. Everyone on the crowded subway is flustered when the train screeched to a halt.
    C. Everyone on the crowded subway was flustered when the train screeched to a halt.
    D. Everyone on the crowded subway become flustered when the train screeched to a halt.

39. Choose the sentence that is communicates an idea clearly.

    A. It is not clear why, but the school has been closed for the day.
    B. Why is not clear, but the school has been closed for the day.
    C. While it is not clear, the school has been closed for the day.
    D. The school being closed for the day is not clear.

40. Choose the sentence that is grammatically correct.

    A. The flight attendant asked the passenger to return his seat to the upright position, shut off his electronics, and to buckle his seatbelt.
    B. The flight attendant asked the passenger to return his seat to the upright position, shut off his electronics, and buckle his seatbelt.
    C. The flight attendant asked the passenger to return his seat to the upright position, to shut off his electronics, and buckle his seatbelt.
    D. The flight attendant asked the passenger to return his seat to the upright position, to be shutting off his electronics, and to buckle his seatbelt.

Beatrice is an office manager who needs to record an out-of-office voicemail message while she is on vacation.

41. Which would be the most professional choice?

    A. Leave your contact information, and I'll be happy to help you when I can.
    B. Please leave your information, and call back if you don't hear from me in a week.
    C. Leave your contact information, and I will get back with you when I have time.
    D. Please leave your information, and I will contact you as soon as I return to the office.

Jack received a call from the human resources department at a company where he has recently interviewed informing him that he did not get the position. However, he wants to write a formal thank you letter to the person who interviewed him.

42. Which of the following is the most professional way to word the opening sentence?

    A. I understand that you had a lot of applicants, but I feel that you missed out on a great employee by not choosing me.
    B. While I know you interviewed a lot of people, you're going to be sorry that you did not give me an opportunity to prove myself.
    C. I appreciate the chance to interview and hope that you will keep me in mind for future opportunities.
    D. Your time and consideration is much appreciated, and I hope you will contact me if the person you chose doesn't work out.

Ms. Diaz is a teacher at an alternative high school for at-risk students. She needs to send out an email to parents whose kids are in danger of not graduating.

43. Which would be the most positive last line?

    A. I would like to thank you in advance for working with me as I take every measure to help your child get back on track.
    B. If you want your child to graduate on time, I strongly suggest you speak with them about getting on track.
    C. I regret to inform you that we must place our focus and attention on our students who are on track to graduate.
    D. At this time, it is highly unlikely that your child will walk the stage in June; therefore, may I suggest summer school?

Lizbeth wants to address the school board about the lack of sufficient recess time at her child's elementary school.

44. Which would be the most effective opening line for her speech?

    A. Ten minutes after lunch is not good enough when it comes to playground time.
    B. How would you like it if your kid only got 10 minutes of playground time at school?
    C. I would like to bring the issue of limited playground time at my child's school to your attention.
    D. Although I doubt any of you will remember this, kids actually need sufficient playground time.

During an Individual Education Plan (IEP) meeting in which the student is present, a parent becomes irate that his child will no longer receive the services he thinks are necessary.

45. Which would be the best way to address his concern?

       A. "Sir, you must calm yourself, especially in front of the child."

       B. "I understand your concern; let's discuss alternatives."

       C. "I am going to have to have you removed if you don't calm down."

       D. "While you have valid concerns, that service just isn't on the table."

NAVAED

1.	B		24.	A
2.	B		25.	D
3.	A		26.	C
4.	A		27.	D
5.	C		28.	A
6.	D		29.	B
7.	B		30.	B
8.	D		31.	A
9.	B		32.	D
10.	A		33.	C
11.	C		34.	A
12.	D		35.	A
13.	A		36.	D
14.	D		37.	C
15.	C		38.	C
16.	B		39.	A
17.	C		40.	B
18.	A		41.	D
19.	B		42.	C
20.	C		43.	A
21.	C		44.	C
22.	B		45.	B
23.	C			

DIRECTIONS: For questions 1–10, select the most appropriate word to complete the sentence.

1. Much to his _____, the student did not get accepted into the college of his choice.

    A. revelry - lively
    B. **chagrin - distress/embarrassment**
    C. confidence - belief in one's abilities
    D. disdain - hatred

2. We felt empathy for the disheveled, _____ homeless man begging for money.

    A. tidy - this is an antonym for *disheveled*
    B. **unkempt – means the same as *disheveled***
    C. orderly - means the same as *tidy*
    D. immaculate - means the same as *tidy*

3. During freshman orientation, the students were feverishly taking _____ 3 notes.

    A. **copious - abundant, plentiful**
    B. verbose - wordy (used more for speech than writing)
    C. loquacious - talkative
    D. scant - minimal, negligible

4. The teacher _____ the class for its _____ behavior on the field trip.

    A. **chastised, unruly - scolded, reprimanded; difficult to control**
    B. commended, unruly - praised; difficult to control
    C. chastised, orderly - scolded; well-behaved
    D. reprimanded, orderly - scolded; well-behaved

5. As she prepared to move into the dorm, it dawned on her that she had _____ too many things.

    A. accounted - considered; regarded
    B. accredited - officially recognized or authorized
    C. **accumulated - acquired an increasing number**
    D. accrued - accumulate or collect funds. This is close in meaning to accumulated, but is more of a technical term for finance

6. The _____ professor refused to grade any assignments that did not follow his exact instructions.

    A. Pompous – arrogant
    B. scrupulous - upstanding; principled. In context, *fastidious* is the better choice
    C. cautious - careful
    D. **fastidious - concerned with accuracy and detail, demanding, nitpicky**

7. _____ is not a good quality in a physician.

    A. resolution - finding a solution to a conflict or problem
    B. <u>arrogance - behaving and believing that you are better than others</u>
    C. fortitude - mental strength
    D. empathy - sharing someone else's feelings

8. When the ambulance arrived, the _____ patient refused to cooperate.

    A. complacent - satisfied with one's current circumstances
    B. submissive - compliant, obedient
    C. indelible - permanent
    D. <u>obstinate - stubborn</u>

9. In a world of conflict, she attempted to be _____.

    A. contentious - likely to cause an argument; controversial
    B. <u>sanguine - optimistic or positive, especially in a bad situation</u>
    C. conducive - making a certain outcome likely
    D. intolerant - bigoted; narrow-minded

10. After much debate, the council members could not reach a _____ at the meeting, forcing them to table the decision.

    A. <u>consensus - agreement</u>
    B. conclusion - end or finish
    C. cessation - being brought to an end
    D. concurrence - simultaneous occurrence of events or circumstances

11. Her list of complaints about the apartment was <u>long; bad view,</u> too noisy, ugly carpet, and small kitchen.

    A. long, bad view,

    B. long (bad view,)

    C. long: bad view,

       Use a colon with an independent clause that is followed by a list.

    D. No change is necessary.

12. <u>Now that he was 18,</u> he thought he didn't need his parents.

    A. Now that he was 18

    B. Now that he was 18;

    C. Now that he was 18:

    D. No change is necessary.

       Use a comma following an introductory phrase.

13. <u>Stop! Shouted</u> the frustrated mother.

    A. "Stop!" shouted

       Dialogue is tricky. When you use an exclamation point or a question mark within the quotation marks, no comma or capitalization is needed following the quote.

    B. "Stop!", shouted

    C. "Stop!" Shouted

    D. No change is necessary.

14. The advisor gave Tim a list of the courses he needed for his <u>program: Macro Economics, Business Law, and Financial Accounting.</u>

    A. Program - Macro Economics, Business Law, and Financial Accounting.

    B. program: macro economics, business law, and financial accounting.

    C. program. Macro Economics, Business Law, and Financial Accounting.

    D. No change is necessary.

       There are two things being tested here: Use a colon with an independent clause followed by a list. In addition, titles of courses are capitalized. Generic names like math, science, and history, however, are not.

15. When he found out he failed the test <u>yet again he decided</u> college was not for him.

    A. yet again; he decided

    B. yet, again, he decided

    C. yet again, he decided

       Use a comma following a dependent clause hooked to an independent clause.

    D. No change is necessary.

16. The <u>tiny diminutive</u> girl was not tall enough for the roller coaster.

    A. tiny, diminutive

    B. <u>diminutive</u>

    Because *diminutive* means the same thing as *tiny,* you need to take one out. Remember to avoid redundancy.

    C. diminutive,

    D. No change is necessary.

17. <u>Unfortunately she forgot</u> the most important part of the birthday celebration: the gift.

    A. She, unfortunately forgot

    B. She unfortunately, forgot

    C. <u>Unfortunately, she forgot</u>

    Introductory words require a comma.

    D. No change is necessary.

18. When the state officials announced huge budget cuts in <u>education administrators, teachers, and parents</u> were livid.

    A. <u>education, administrators, teachers, and parents</u>

    A comma is needed after the introductory phrase, *When the state officials announced huge budget cuts in education,*

    B. education, administrators teachers and parents

    C. education, administrators and teachers, parents

    D. No change is necessary.

19. His feelings were hurt <u>when the chocolates he gave the girl were rejected.</u>

    A. when the girl rejected the chocolates which he gave her.

    B. <u>when the girl rejected the chocolates that he gave her.</u>

    Active voice (*the girl rejected*) is usually preferred over passive voice (*were rejected).* Although A is a very close answer choice, nonrestrictive clauses using *which* must be set off with commas.

    C. when the girl rejected the chocolates, that he gave her.

    D. No change is necessary.

20. The CFO warned his staff <u>not to talk at the media</u> about the incident.

    A. not to talk for the media

    B. to not speak to the media

    C. <u>not to speak to the media</u>

    Use the process of elimination if you are stuck. Eliminate A because it changes the meaning of the sentence. Eliminate B because the negative is formed by adding *not* before the infinitive (*to speak*). Eliminate D because *at* is not the correct preposition for talk.

    D. No change is necessary.

21. Determine the purpose of the parentheses.

    Marisa (who was busy texting her friend) ignored her mother's request to empty the dishwasher.

    A. to clarify who ignored the mother's request
    B. to introduce a new person into the situation
    C. **to enclose information that clarifies the situation**
    The phrase inside the parentheses (*who was busy texting her friend*) gives additional information about the situation. While B may seem logical, but the phrase is more about what Marisa was doing while she ignored her mother instead of introducing a new person.
    D. to add humor to the tense situation

22. Determine the purpose of the apostrophe.

    The baby's favorite toy was misplaced.

    A. to form a contraction
    B. **to indicate that the toy belonged to the baby**
    In this sentence, there is one baby who has a favorite toy. The *'s* shows possession. Eliminate A because *baby is* does not make sense. Eliminate C because an apostrophe is not needed to make the word *child* plural. Eliminate D because multiple children would not be *babies'*.
    C. to make the word *baby* plural
    D. to show that more than one baby owned the toy

23. Determine the purpose of the parentheses.

    The teammates (accompanied by their coach) had a celebratory dinner after their victory.

    A. to include the coach as part of the subject
    B. to show that the coach was an afterthought
    C. **to clarify that the coach also attended the dinner**
    Parentheses can be used to add information that clarifies but is not essential to the sentence and to show that the information within the parentheses is not as important— almost an afterthought. However, information included in parentheses is NOT included in the subject, making A incorrect.
    D. to diminish the role that the coach played

24. Choose the sentence in which the apostrophe is accurately placed.

    A. <u>The boys decided it would be funny to steal the girls' books as payback for telling the teacher they cheated on the last test.</u>

        Because there are multiple girls, the apostrophe needs to come after the *s* to show that multiple girls possessed the books.

    B. The boys' decided it would be funny to steal the girls books as payback for telling the teacher they cheated on the last test.

    C. The boys decided it would be funny to steal the girls's books as payback for telling the teacher they cheated on the last test.

    D. The boy's decided it would be funny to steal the girls books as payback for telling the teacher they cheated on the last test.

25. Choose the sentence in which the parentheses are accurately placed.

    A. Joey and (his mother) continued to drive well after he realized they were lost.

    B. Joey and his mother continued (to drive) well after he realized they were lost.

    C. Joey and his mother (continued to) drive well after he realized they were lost.

    D. <u>Joey (and his mother) continued to drive well after he realized he was lost.</u>

        Information enclosed in parentheses is NOT part of the subject. *Joey* is the subject, making D a grammatically correct sentence.

(1) "What do you want to be when you grow up?" (2) It's a question that adults commonly ask school-aged children. (3) Some of the traditional answers include: doctor, nurse, firefighter, teacher, and police officer. (4) However, students today may have their sights set on more a more technical career such as social media architect, data scientist, computer software engineer, or network systems analyst. (5) And, as technology continues to race forward at lightning speed, new job titles will be created to support consumer demand. (6) The simple question, "What do you want to be when you grow up?" may have some answers that have adults scratching their heads.

26. What is the best placement for the sentence below?

    Many of these careers are familiar to kids who have grown up with technology but not so familiar to many adults.

    A. before sentence 6
    B. after sentence 3
    C. after sentence 4

    For these types of questions, read the paragraph with the sentence in each place. Because it includes the phrase *these careers,* this sentence needs to come after the sentence that addresses specific careers. However, after sentence 3 (B) does not work as the sentence refers to technology. The careers listed in sentence 3 are not technology-focused careers, making C the best option.

    D. before sentence 3

(1) Many worry that children are getting too much screen time. (2) In the past, television was about the only screen parents needed to monitor. (3) However, with technology, children are exposed to screens not only through television but also through phones, tablets, in-car entertainment centers, and computers. (4) How much is too much? (5) Not everyone agrees, but many experts say children under 2 should have no screen time, and children over 2 should have no more than 2 hours per day of screen time.

27. Which would be the best concluding sentence after sentence 5?

    A. Whether or not you agree with these strict guidelines, you should always do what the experts suggest.
    B. Although these recommendations are unrealistic, you should consider them when deciding on how much screen time to give a child.
    C. If you want to be a good parent, you need to follow these expert recommendations regardless of how unrealistic they may seem.
    D. While many would argue these guidelines are not realistic, they do bring attention to the need to monitor and limit a child's daily screen time.

    Eliminate A because it uses *always.* Remember, *always, never, only,* etc. are generally too extreme. Eliminate B because it is an opinion that the recommendations are unrealistic. C has a condescending tone that does not fit the tone of the rest of the passage. D is the best choice because it acknowledges the opposing side while pointing out the issue being addressed.

(1) Many retirees chose to spend their golden years in warmer climates. (2) Florida and California have been popular options for these folks. (3) However, arid Arizona has grown as a favorite place to retire. (4) In addition, Arizona generally avoids natural disasters and never gets hit with hurricanes or earthquakes. (5) Beyond the sunny, warm, and dry climate, Arizona is also an affordable place to live. (6) No wonder it has become a retirement destination for many.

28. Which of the following is the best title for this passage?

    A. **Arizona Attracts More and More Retirees**

        This title best summarizes the information in the passage. Eliminate B because although Florida is mentioned, the article as a whole does not focus on Arizona beating out Florida as a retirement destination. C contradicts information in the passage. D alludes to a problem.

    B. Arizona Beating Out Florida as a Retirement Destination

    C. Arizona Heat Too Much for the Aging Population

    D. Arizona Faces the Heat as a Retirement Community

(1) There is a national crisis looming, one that has the potential to affect millions of American children. (2) While this assessment may sound dramatic, the national teacher shortage already affects students across our country. (3) But, many current teachers will attest that increasing workloads, unrealistic expectations, and low salaries are to blame for veteran teachers calling it quits. (4) Students are packed into classrooms when schools do not have enough teachers to keep class sizes low, and in worst case scenarios, kids are held in auditoriums or gyms when there are no teachers at all. (5) Unfortunately, there is no single factor causing this. (6) Decreasing the workload and increasing pay would certainly go a long way to retaining current teachers and attracting new ones.

29. What is the best sentence order to provide a logical sequence of ideas?

    A. 6, 1, 2, 3, 4, 5

    B. **1, 2, 4, 5, 3, 6**

        These logical order questions are tough, especially when two of the choices start with the same two numbers! Eliminate A and D because sentence 6 is not a good opening sentence for the paragraph. Sentence 2 needs to come after sentence 1 because the "assessment" it mentions refers to the "crisis" in sentence 1. When weighing the last two options, the order of the sentences in B makes for a clear paragraph.

    C. 1, 3, 2, 5, 4, 6

    D. 6, 5, 2, 3, 1, 4

(1) All over America, vending machines at schools have been emptied of any drinks with sugar. (2) Those sweet and calorie-laden cans of soda, sports drinks, and flavored water were replaced with "diet" versions, purportedly because they are healthier options. (3) However, how healthy is it for kids to consume these artificial sweeteners on a daily basis? (4) Over the years, research has shown that sugar substitutes can increase sugar cravings. (5) All of this raises an important question: Have the changes to vending machine offerings made kids healthier or just replaced one unhealthy option with another?

30. Which sentence would fit best between sentences 4 and 5?

    A. This, unfortunately, will just cause obesity rates to rise among our children.

    B. <u>Research has also linked daily use of these products to certain health issues.</u>

        A and C both jump to hasty conclusions that cannot be proven to be accurate, so eliminate them as answers. The tone in C is too casual to match the objective tone of the rest of the passage. B is the only choice that ties the two sentences together and matches the tone.

    C. However, nutritional guidelines are always changing, so who knows.

    D. So, kids who drink diet sodas are less likely to exercise and thus gain weight.

31. Choose the sentence that is grammatically correct.

    A. <u>**Many will agree that public servants such as nurses, firefighters, police officers, social workers, and teachers need to be paid better salaries.**</u>

    The colon is misused in B. No colon is needed after *such as,* so eliminate C. Finally, the way the careers are organized in D is not ideal.

    B. Many will agree that public servants: such as nurses; firefighters; police officers; social workers; and teachers need to be paid better salaries.

    C. Many will agree that public servants such as: nurses, firefighters, police officers, social workers, and teachers need to be paid better salaries.

    D. Many will agree that public servants such as nurses, firefighters and police officers, social workers and teachers need to be paid better salaries.

32. Choose the sentence that is grammatically correct.

    A. Cyber-bullying has become an issue, with the spike in social media use.

    B. Cyber-bullying has become an issue, because of the spike in social media use.

    C. Cyber-bullying has become an issue; with the spike in social media use.

    D. <u>**With the spike in social media use, cyber-bullying has become an issue.**</u>

    Commas are not necessary before *with* or *because,* eliminating A and B. The semicolon in C is also misused. The use of an introductory clause and independent clause separated by a comma is the correct choice.

33. Choose the sentence that is grammatically correct.

    A. The patients in the medical trial received compensation for they're participation.

    B. The patients in the medical trial received compensation for there participation.

    C. <u>**The patients in the medical trial received compensation for their participation.**</u>

    When looking at the three forms of *there-their-they're*, only C is used correctly as a plural possessive pronoun to match the plural antecedent (*patients*). The use of *his or her* in D is incorrect because they are singular possessive pronouns and the antecedent (*patients*) is plural.

    D. The patients in the medical trial received compensation for his or her participation.

34. Choose the sentence that is grammatically correct.

    A. <u>**With fuel prices plummeting, many are perplexed by the increase in airline ticket prices.**</u>

    A is the only choice that is clearly stated. Who is perplexed by the increase of airline ticket prices? Many are. Why? Because fuel prices are plummeting.

    B. With fuel prices plummeting, the price increase in airline tickets is perplexing.

    C. With the price of fuel plummeting, increases in airline tickets perplexes.

    D. With the price of fuel plummeting, increased airline tickets remains perplexed.

35. Choose the sentence that is grammatically correct.

    A. **He was the only one in the class who read the assigned chapters.**

    Who read the assigned chapters? He did. If the answer were *him*, D would be correct. You would not say "Him read the assigned chapters" so eliminate that as a choice. *That* and *which* are used with things, not people.

    B. He was the only one in the class that read the assigned chapters.

    C. He was the only one in the class which read the assigned chapters.

    D. He was the only one in the class whom read the assigned chapters.

36. Choose the sentence that is grammatically correct.

    A. As each hour passed, the mother's concern increased that her son wasn't home yet.

    B. With each passing hour, the mother became concerned increasingly that her son wasn't home yet.

    C. As each hour passed by, the concern of the mother increased that her son wasn't home yet.

    D. **With each passing hour, the mother became increasingly concerned that her son wasn't home yet.**

    This is the choice that is worded clearly. The others are confusing.

37. Choose the sentence that is grammatically correct.

    A. The use of cell phones and computers have been prohibited.

    B. The use of cell phones and computers were prohibited.

    C. **The use of cell phones and computers is prohibited.**

    Be on the lookout for this little trick. The test makers will put a prepositional phrase (*of cell phones*) between the subject (*use*) and predicate *(is)* to throw you off. *The use is prohibited* is correct subject/verb agreement. *The use have been* is incorrect (A). Ditto for *The use were* (B) and *The use are* (D).

    D. The use of cell phones and computers are prohibited.

38. Choose the sentence that is grammatically correct.

    A. Everyone on the crowded subway were flustered when the train screeched to a halt.

    B. Everyone on the crowded subway is flustered when the train screeched to a halt.

    C. **Everyone on the crowded subway was flustered when the train screeched to a halt.**

    This is another subject/verb agreement question with the pesky prepositional phrase stuck between the subject and the predicate! *Everyone was flustered* and *Everyone is flustered* could both be correct. However, this question addresses another issue— tense. The subject/verb agreement alone in B could be correct except that the train *screeched* to a halt, so you would use the past tense *was.*

    D. Everyone on the crowded subway become flustered when the train screeched to a halt.

39. Choose the sentence that is grammatically correct.

    A. **It is not clear why, but the school has been closed for the day.**

    This is the only option that is worded following conventional English syntax.

    B. Why is not clear, but the school has been closed for the day.

    C. While it is not clear, the school has been closed for the day.

    D. The school being closed for the day is not clear.

40. Choose the sentence that is grammatically correct.

    A. The flight attendant asked the passenger to return his seat to the upright position, shut off his electronics, and to buckle his seatbelt.

    B. <u>The flight attendant asked the passenger to return his seat to the upright position, shut off his electronics, and buckle his seatbelt.</u>

    This is the only choice with parallel structure (*return his seat, shut off his electronics, buckle his seatbelt*).

    C. The flight attendant asked the passenger to return his seat to the upright position, to shut off his electronics, and buckle his seatbelt.

    D. The flight attendant asked the passenger to return his seat to the upright position, tobe shutting off his electronics, and to buckle his seatbelt.

Beatrice is an office manager who needs to record an out-of-office voicemail message while she is on vacation.

41. Which would be the most professional choice?

   A. Leave your contact information, and I'll be happy to help you when I can.
   B. Please leave your information, and call back if you don't hear from me in a week.
   C. <u>Leave your contact information, and I will get back with you when I have time.</u>
   D. **Please leave your information, and I will contact you as soon as I return to the office.**
      This is the most professional choice. *When I can* in A and *when I have time* in C are dismissive. B puts the responsibility back on the caller, which is not professional.

Jack received a call from the human resources department at a company where he has recently interviewed informing him that he did not get the position. However, he wants to write a formal thank you letter to the person who interviewed him.

42. Which of the following is the most professional way to word the opening sentence?

   A. I understand that you had a lot of applicants, but I feel that you missed out on a great employee by not choosing me.
   B. While I know you interviewed a lot of people, you're going to be sorry that you did not give me an opportunity to prove myself.
   C. <u>**I appreciate the chance to interview and hope that you will keep me in mind for future opportunities.**</u>
      This option is professional and lets the interviewer know Jack is still interested in working for the company in the future. D is close, but the word choice *if the person you chose doesn't work out* is too informal and presumptuous.
   D. Your time and consideration is much appreciated, and I hope you will contact me if the person you chose doesn't work out.

Ms. Diaz is a teacher at an alternative high school for at-risk students. She needs to send out an email to parents whose kids are in danger of not graduating.

43. Which would be the positive last line?

   A. <u>**I would like to thank you in advance for working with me as I take every measure to help your child get back on track.**</u>
      This option is the most diplomatic way to broach a touchy situation and get the point across. It lets the parents know that she wants to work with them and is not blaming anyone. B is too forceful and bossy. C indicates she is giving up on the student. D assumes failure, which as a teacher, you never want to do.
   B. If you want your child to graduate on time, I strongly suggest you speak with them about getting on track.
   C. I regret to inform you that we must place our focus and attention on our students who are on track to graduate.
   D. At this time, it is highly unlikely that your child will walk the stage in June; therefore, may I suggest summer school?

Lizbeth wants to address the school board about the lack of sufficient recess time at her child's elementary school.

44. Which would be the effective opening line for her speech?

    A. Ten minutes after lunch is not good enough when it comes to playground time.
    B. How would you like it if your kid only got 10 minutes of playground time at school?
    C. **I would like to bring the issue of limited playground time at my child's school to your attention.**

       This clearly states the problem in a nonconfrontational manner. The other choices may put the schoolboard on the defensive, which is never a good thing to do when seeking help and cooperation for an issue.
    D. Although I doubt any of you will remember this, kids actually need sufficient playground time.

During an Individual Education Plan (IEP) meeting in which the student is present, a parent becomes irate that his child will no longer receive the services he thinks are necessary.

45. Which would be the best way to address his concern?

    A. Sir, you must calm yourself, especially in front of the child.
    B. **I understand your concern; let's discuss alternatives.**

       This is the only option that refrains from being confrontational, acknowledges the concern, and offers compromise.
    C. I am going to have to have you removed if you don't calm down.
    D. While you have valid concerns, that service just isn't on the table.

DIRECTIONS: Choose the option that corrects an error in the underlined portion(s). If no error exists, choose "No change is necessary."

1. The advisor gave Tim a list of the courses he needed for his <u>program: Macro Economics, Business Law, and Financial Accounting.</u>

    A. Program - Macro Economics, Business Law, and Financial Accounting.

    B. program: macro economics, business law, and financial accounting.

    C. program. Macro Economics, Business Law, and Financial Accounting.

    D. No change is necessary.

DIRECTIONS: Choose the option that corrects an error in the underlined portion(s). If no error exists, choose "No change is necessary."

2. My friend, her dog, and I went for a ride in my new car, and <u>she</u> chewed through one of the seat belts.

    A. my friend

    B. her dog

    C. they

    D. No change is necessary.

DIRECTIONS: Choose the best word to complete the sentence in context.

3. During freshman orientation, the students were feverishly taking _____ notes.

    A. copious

    B. verbose

    C. loquacious

    D. scant

DIRECTIONS: Choose the option that corrects an error in the underlined portion(s). If no error exists, choose "No change is necessary."

4. When it was clear that the storm was <u>eminent,</u> we <u>had</u> to decide <u>whether</u> to stay where we were or go to a shelter.

    A. imminent

    B. have

    C. weather

    D. No change is necessary

DIRECTIONS: Choose the best word to complete the sentence in context.

5. We felt empathy for the disheveled,_____homeless man begging for money.

    A. tidy

    B. unkempt

    C. disorderly

    D. immaculate

DIRECTIONS: Choose the best word to complete the sentence in context.

6. As she prepared to move into the dorm, it dawned on her that she had_____ too many things.

    A. accounted

    B. accredited

    C. accumulated

    D. accrued

DIRECTIONS: Choose the option that corrects an error in the underlined portion(s). If no error exists, choose "No change is necessary."

7. When the state officials announced huge budget cuts in education administrators, teachers, and parents were livid.

    A. education, administrators, teachers, and parents

    B. education, administrators teachers and parents

    C. education, administrators and teachers, parents

    D. No change is necessary.

8. Choose the sentence with no errors.

    A. The team was upset when they were eliminated from the finals.

    B. The team was upset when it was eliminated from the finals.

    C. The team members was upset when they were eliminated from the finals.

    D. Each individual on the team was upset when it was eliminated from the finals.

9. Choose the sentence with no errors.

    A. The band sold their CDs after the concert.

    B. The band sold they're CDs after the concert.

    C. The band sold its CDs after the concert.

    D. The band sold it's CDs after the concert.

DIRECTIONS: Choose the best word to complete the sentence in context.

10. The student was suspended in_____with the district's Code of Conduct.

    A. correspondence

    B. accountability

    C. concurrence

    D. accordance

DIRECTIONS: Choose the best word to complete the sentence in context.

11. The_____professor refused to grade any assignments that did not follow his exact instructions.

    A. pompous

    B. scrupulous

    C. cautious

    D. fastidious

DIRECTIONS: Choose the option that corrects an error in the underlined portion(s). If no error exists, choose "No change is necessary."

12. The young boy liked his first-grade teacher, Ms. Young, better <u>then</u> his second grade teacher because <u>Ms. Young</u> was more <u>complimentary</u> of him.

    A. than

    B. she

    C. complementary

    D. No change is necessary

DIRECTIONS: Choose the option that corrects an error in the underlined portion(s). If no error exists, choose "No change is necessary."

13. The school decided to <u>eliminate</u> the <u>coarse due</u> to lack of interest.

    A. illuminate

    B. course

    C. do

    D. No change is necessary

DIRECTIONS: Choose the option that corrects an error in the underlined portion(s). If no error exists, choose "No change is necessary."

14. The <u>stationery</u> bikes at the gym <u>have been broken</u> for three months, creating <u>an</u> extremely long wait for the other machines.

    A. stationary

    B. have been broke

    C. a

    D. No change is necessary

NAVAED

DIRECTIONS: Read the passage, then answer the question below. Intentional errors may be included.

(1) Too many times, college students neglect to realize that college courses require more work outside of class than during class. (2) This is quite a shock for students who are used to completing most of their academic work in a classroom. (3) High schools need to do a better job of preparing students for college. (4) Developing time management skills is vital to success at the college level. (5) Although it's never too late for students to learn to effectively use their time, high school is the best time to hone this important skill.

15. Which sentence does NOT contribute to the logical progression of this passage?

    A. sentence 1

    B. sentence 2

    C. sentence 3

    D. sentence 4

16. Choose the sentence with no errors.

    A. Out of the three choices, Katrina liked the red car better.

    B. Out of the three choices, Katrina liked the red car best.

    C. Out of the three choices, Katrina liked the red car more.

DIRECTIONS: Read the passage, then answer the question below. Intentional errors may be included.

(1) There is a national crisis looming, one that has the potential to affect millions of American children. (2) While this assessment may sound dramatic, the national teacher shortage already affects students across our country. (3) But, many current teachers will attest that increasing work loads, unrealistic expectations, and low salaries are to blame for veteran teachers calling it quits. (4) Students are packed into classrooms when schools do not have enough teachers to keep class sizes low, and in worst case scenarios, kids are held in auditoriums or gyms when there are no teachers at all. (5) Unfortunately, there is no single factor causing this. (6) Decreasing the work load and increasing pay would certainly go a long way to retaining current teachers and attracting new ones.

17. What is the best sentence order to provide a logical sequence of ideas?

    A. 6, 1, 2, 3, 4, 5

    B. 1, 2, 4, 5, 3, 6

    C. 1, 3, 2, 5, 4, 6

    D. 6, 5, 2, 3, 1, 4

DIRECTIONS: Choose the best word to complete the sentence in context.

18. Pretending a problem doesn't exist won't help the situation; instead, it will only_____it.

    A. exacerbate

    B. antagonize

    C. suppress

    D. exasperate

DIRECTIONS: Read the following scenario and answer the question that follows each.

Katherine is a volunteer basketball coach for the local YMCA. She needs to draft a letter that spells out the expectations for the participants and their parents.

19. Which would be the most appropriate closing line for Katherine's letter?

    A. I am looking forward to a great season and want to thank you in advance for your cooperation.

    B. This will be a great season if everyone cooperates and follows the guidelines set forth in this letter.

    C. I know that everyone thinks their child is special, but I believe that all of the children are special.

    D. I appreciate your cooperation and would also like to remind you that as a volunteer, I don't get paid.

20. Choose the sentence with no errors.

    A. The principle was livid when she found out a teacher at her school had been selling pencils for a personal profit.

    B. The principle was livid when she found out a teacher at her school has been selling pencils for a personal profit.

    C. The principal was livid when she found out a teacher at her school had been selling pencils for a personal profit.

DIRECTIONS: Choose the option that corrects an error in the underlined portion(s). If no error exists, choose "No change is necessary."

21. If the manager wants to boost <u>moral</u>, she should consider praising her <u>employees more often than she currently does</u>.

    A. morale

    B. employee's

    C. more

    D. No change is necessary.

22. DIRECTIONS: Choose the sentence with no errors.

    A. The professor's book was more well-received by the general public than by his colleagues.

    B. The professors' book was better well-received by the general public then by his colleagues.

    C. The professor's book was best received by the general public then by his colleagues.

    D. The professor's book was better received by the general public than by his colleagues.

23. DIRECTIONS: Choose the sentence with no errors.

    A. The use of cell phones and computers have been prohibited.

    B. The use of cell phones and computers were prohibited.

    C. The use of cell phones and computers is prohibited.

    D. The use of cell phones and computers are prohibited.

24. DIRECTIONS: Choose the sentence with no errors.

    A. Everyone on the crowded subway were flustered when the train screeched to a halt.

    B. Everyone on the crowded subway is flustered when the train screeched to a halt.

    C. Everyone on the crowded subway was flustered when the train screeched to a halt.

    D. Everyone on the crowded subway become flustered when the train screeched to a halt.

DIRECTIONS: Choose the best word to complete the sentence in context.

25. After their mother's death, the_____siblings fought over who would inherit her estate.

    A. factious

    B. fastidious

    C. factitious

    D. fractional

DIRECTIONS: Choose the option that corrects an error in the underlined portion(s). If no error exists, choose "No change is necessary."

26. His course demeanor was evident as he barreled through the emergency room doors, demanding to be seen before the other patients.

    A. coarse

    B. threw

    C. patience

    D. No change is necessary

27. DIRECTIONS: Choose the sentence with no errors in structure.

    A. When the weather became threatening, they decided to bring the boat in and seeking shelter.

    B. When the weather became threatening, they decided to bring the boat in and seek shelter.

    C. When the weather became threatening, they decided to bring the boat in and sought shelter.

28. DIRECTIONS: Choose the sentence with correct parallel structure.

    A. The store manager was growing impatient with her employees' not caring, constantly lateness, and standing around when there was work to be done.

    B. The store manager was growing impatient with her employees' lack of caring, lack of promptness, and how lazy they were.

    C. The store manager was growing impatient with her employees' apathy, tardiness, and laziness.

29. DIRECTIONS: Choose the sentence with correct modifier placement.

    A. Her car broke down on the side of the road while calling roadside assistance.

    B. She was calling roadside assistance while her car was breaking down on the side of the road.

    C. Calling roadside assistance, her car broke down on the side of the road.

    D. When her car broke down on the side of the road, she called roadside assistance.

30. DIRECTIONS: Choose the sentence with no errors in structure.

    A. The student's father was displeased when he learned he had failed the first semester.

    B. The student's father was displeased when he learned his son had failed the first semester.

    C. The father of the student was displeased when his son had failed the first semester.

    D. The father of the student was displeased when he failed the first semester.

31. DIRECTIONS: Choose the sentence with no errors in structure.

    A. It is important that you follow the directions carefully when you're handling the chemicals.

    B. It is important that you follow the directions carefully when your handling the chemicals.

    C. It is important that you follow the directions carefully handling the chemicals.

DIRECTIONS: Choose the option that corrects an error in the underlined portion(s). If no error exists, choose "No change is necessary."

32. The graduate's mother handed him some stationary and told him to write thank you notes for his gifts.

    A. graduates

    B. stationery

    C. right

    D. No change is necessary

33. DIRECTIONS: Choose the sentence with correct parallel structure.

    A. The new restaurant offered meals that are fresh, healthy and were cooked quickly.

    B. The new restaurant offered meals that are fresher, healthy, and quick.

    C. The new restaurant offers meals that are freshest, healthier, and made quickly.

    D. The new restaurant offers meals that are fresh, healthy, and quick.

34. DIRECTIONS: Choose the sentence with correct parallel structure.

    A. After his heart attack, his doctor told him to avoid fatty foods, beginning an exercise program, and scheduling regular checkups.

    B. After his heart attack, his doctor was telling him to avoid fatty foods, begin an exercise program, and scheduled regular checkups.

    C. After his heart attack, his doctor told him to avoid fatty foods, begin an exercise program, and schedule regular checkups.

    D. After his heart attack, his doctor was telling him to avoid fatty foods, exercise, and regular checkups.

DIRECTIONS: Read the following scenarios and answer the questions that follow.

A parent is writing a letter to the school board about the lack of sufficient recess time at her child's elementary school.

35. What is the best opening line for her letter?

    A. Ten minutes after lunch is not good enough when it comes to playground time.

    B. How would you like it if your child only got 10 minutes of playground time at school?

    C. I would like to bring the issue of limited playground time at my child's school to your attention.

    D. Although I doubt any of you will remember this, kids actually need sufficient playground time.

Ms. Diaz is a teacher at an alternative high school for at-risk students. She needs to send out an email to parents whose kids are in danger of not graduating.

36. Which would be the best closing line for her message?

    A. I would like to thank you in advance for working with me, as I take every measure to help your child get back on track.

    B. If you want your child to graduate on time, I strongly suggest you speak with them about getting on track.

    C. I regret to inform you that we must place our focus and attention on our students who are on track to graduate.

    D. At this time, it is highly unlikely that your child will walk the stage in June, therefore, may I suggest summer school?

37. DIRECTIONS: Choose the sentence with no errors.

    A. I didn't know which was worst: the long line or the person talking loudly behind me.

    B. I didn't know which was worse: the long line or the person talking loudly behind me.

    C. I didn't know what was worse: the long line or the person talking loudly behind me.

    D. I didn't know what was worst: the long line or the person talking loudly behind me.

DIRECTIONS: Read the passage below and answer the questions that follow. There may be intentional errors in the passage.

(1) Many people love the game of baseball. (2) Fans come out in droves to hear the crack of the bat, cheer for every run their team makes, and boo the umpire when he made a bad call. (3) Of course, the ballpark food also draws fans to the games. (4) Unfortunately, it's unhealthy fare. (5) Foods like hot dogs, peanuts, and popcorn are staples of most ballpark concession stands. (6) Whether fans come for the sport, the food, or both, one thing is certain: baseball is still a popular pastime.

38. Which sentence has an error in verb tense?

    A. sentence 6

    B. sentence 5

    C. sentence 2

    D. sentence 1

39. Which sentence is off topic?

    A. sentence 5

    B. sentence 4

    C. sentence 3

    D. sentence 2

40. Refer to sentences 1, 2, 3. Which is the BEST order for these sentences?

    A. 1, 2, 3

    B. 2, 1, 3

    C. 3, 2, 1

    D. 1, 3, 2

1. D	9. C	17. B	25. A	33. D
2. B	10. D	18. A	26. A	34. C
3. A	11. D	19. A	27. B	35. C
4. A	12. A	20. C	28. C	36. A
5. B	13. B	21. A	29. D	37. B
6. C	14. A	22. D	30. B	38. C
7. A	15. C	23. C	31. A	39. B
8. B	16. B	24. C	32. B	40. A

1. **D**. No change is necessary. A colon is the appropriate punctuation mark to use before a list. Since the courses are titles, not general names, they need to be capitalized.

2. **B**. The antecedent for "she" is not clear. Is it the friend or the dog that chewed through the seatbelt? When it is unclear, avoid pronouns.

3. **A**. Copious, or abundant, is the best choice. The context clue *feverishly* hints that the students are moving quickly and frantically, so it is unlikely they are taking scant notes (D). *Verbose* (B) and *loquacious* (C) both mean being unnecessarily wordy, so eliminate those.

4. **A**. When faced with these types of questions, look at each underlined element very carefully. Even if you don't know what *eminent* and *imminent* mean, you can eliminate *have* (B) because it doesn't match the verb tense of the remainder of the sentence, and you can eliminate *weather* (C) easily. *Imminent* means "inevitable, or about to happen," making it the best choice.

5. **B**. *Unkempt* is the most accurate choice. *Disheveled* is the context clue to lead you to the answer. Using this clue helps you eliminate the antonyms in choices A and D. *Disorderly* (C) is meant to be a distractor, but it doesn't quite fit because it has two meanings and implies the man is being unruly.

6. **C**. *Accumulated* means "to collect or acquire," making it the best choice. *Accrued* (D) is close, but generally refers to money or benefits.

7. **A**. A comma is needed after the dependent clause, *When the state officials announced huge budget cuts,* as well as in between each item in the series.

8. **B**. *Team* is a collective noun and therefore an entity, not a person. It is confusing because a team is made up of people, but all together is considered a thing. The other choices either have the wrong pronoun for team or incorrect subject/verb agreement.

9. **C**. See #8. If it were the members of the band, *their* would be the correct pronoun. B and D are incorrect because they are contractions, not possessive pronouns.

10. **D**. *Accordance* means "in a manner conforming with." *Concurrence* (C) is meant to be the distractor, but that refers to being in agreement or when two things happen at the same time, so it doesn't quite make sense.

11. **D**. One of the meanings of *fastidious* is "to be very concerned about accuracy and detail," making it the best choice. *Scrupulous* (B) has two meanings and generally is used to refer to morals.

12. **A**. Use than, not then, with comparatives (better than, more than). On another note, know the difference between commonly confused words such as *complimentary* (praise) and *complementary* (compatible).

13. **B**. *Coarse* means "rough" and is not the correct word to use here. Replace with *course*.

14. **A**. *Stationary* means "fixed; not movable." *Stationery* is writing paper.

15. **C**. These can be hard to pick out. Read the paragraph, eliminating the sentence for each choice. You will see that sentence 3 is the only one that is not vital for the paragraph. It gets off topic by changing the focus from the students to the high schools.

16. **B**. When dealing with comparatives and superlatives, remember that *better* is used for two items, and *best* is used for more than two. *More* is used as such: She liked the red car more than the blue one.

17. **B**. Eliminate A and D because sentence 6 is a better conclusion than introduction. Sentence 2 needs to come after sentence one because of the dependent clause, *While this assessment may sound dramatic.* It doesn't work anywhere else.

18. **A**. *Exacerbate* fits better in the context. You *antagonize* and *exasperate* a person, not a situation, eliminating B and D. *Suppress* is an antonym of these words.

19. **A**. Professional letters and emails need to remain positive. It's easy to insert an unintended tone in written communication. Thanking people in advance for their cooperation keeps it positive and doesn't put conditions on what will make a great season like B does. C has a condescending and insulting tone, and D is already making excuses.

20. **C.** This is the only choice that uses the proper version of the commonly confused homonyms *principal/principle.*

21. **A.** *Morale* is the proper word to describe the feelings of a group.

22. **D.** When in doubt, go with the answer choice that is the shortest, most concise way to say something. It was better received by these people than by those people. *Better well-received* and *more well-received* are redundant.

23. **C.** When figuring out subject/verb agreement, get rid of the prepositional phrase(s) that often separate the subject from the predicate. *The use is prohibited.* None of the others work.

24. **C.** This is the only choice that satisfies the correct subject verb agreement (Everyone was) and the verb tense consistent with the rest of the sentence.

25. **A.** *Factious* has to do with contention or being quarrelsome.

26. **A.** Remember, *coarse* means "rough" and can be applied to someone's personality. *Course* is a path or program of study.

27. **B.** Match up the verb tense to *bring:* to bring and to seek.

28. **C.** This is a parallel structure question. The only one that keeps a consistent structure is C, which uses the noun versions of the words.

29. **D.** This is the only choice that places the modifier in a way that is not confusing. A and C make it seem like the car is calling roadside assistance while B implies she was calling as her car was breaking down.

30. **B.** The only choice where the antecedent is clearly defined and the reader knows who failed the test is B.

31. **A.** The use of the contraction of *you are, you're* is the correct choice here.

32. **B.** Use the version of the homonym, *stationary/stationery* that refers to the writing materials.

33. **D.** This is the only choice that keeps a consistent, or parallel, structure when referring to the meals: fresh, healthy, and quick.

34. **C.** This is the only choice that keeps a consistent, or parallel structure when discussing the doctor's directives: **avoid** fatty foods, **begin** an exercise program, and **schedule** regular checkups.

35. **C.** This choice is the only one with a professional, objective tone. It simply brings the issue to light and serves as a call to action for the school board.

36. **A.** Again, this choice is professional and avoids blaming anyone—the child, the parent, or the teacher. It assumes that everyone will work as a team to help the child. The others are condescending at best or write the child off at worst.

37. **B.** When given a choice between a set number of things or items, *which* is correct. When the number of items or things is unclear, *what* is more appropriate.

38. **C.** Sentence 2 has incorrect verb tense: *he* **made** *a bad call* should be *he* **makes** *a bad call* to be consistent with the best of the sentence.

39. **B.** Because the idea presented in sentence 4 is never developed, it is unnecessary for the paragraph.

40. **A.** The order of the sentences is most logical as is.

1. DIRECTIONS: Choose the sentence with no errors in structure.

    A. When she witnessed an accident, she was driving.

    B. She was driving down the road and she witnessed an accident.

    C. While she was driving down the road, she witnessed an accident.

DIRECTIONS: Considering the context, choose the word that best completes the sentence below.

2. The thunderstorm could not have happened at a more_____time than it did; we had to go into our meeting soaking wet.

    A. ideal

    B. inopportune

    C. auspicious

    D. benign

DIRECTIONS: Choose the option that corrects an error in the underlined portion(s). If no error exists, choose "No change is necessary."

3. Considering their contentious past, Sheila did not necessarily believe Lisa's complement.

    A. there

    B. passed

    C. compliment

    D. No change is necessary.

4. DIRECTIONS: Choose the sentence with no conventional errors.

    A. The couple had to decide which was most important; a vacation or a new house.

    B. The couple had to decide what was most important: a vacation or a new house.

    C. The couple had to decide what was more important; a vacation or a new house.

    D. The couple had to decide which was more important: a vacation or a new house.

5. DIRECTIONS: Choose the sentence with no conventional errors.

    A. The menu had so many great options, but she finally settled on a Cuban sandwich, one of her favorites.

    B. The menu had so many great options, but she finally settled on a cuban sandwich, one of her favorites.

    C. The menu had so many great options, but she finally settled on a Cuban Sandwich, one of her favorites.

6. DIRECTIONS: Choose the sentence with no conventional errors.

   a. The thought of coming home to a messy house drived her crazy.

   b. The thought of coming home to a messy house drove her crazy.

   c. The thought of coming home to a messy house driven her crazy.

DIRECTIONS: Choose the option that corrects an error in the underlined portion(s). If no error exists, choose "No change is necessary."

7. Tina <u>was surprised</u> when the road <u>reached</u> a dead-end because she <u>misses</u> the sign a mile back.

   A. were surprised

   B. reaches

   C. missed

   D. No change is necessary.

8. DIRECTIONS: Choose the sentence with no conventional errors.

   A. Ben had come to know his teacher very well, he would miss her when he moved next month.

   B. Ben had come to know his teacher very well: he would miss her when he moved next month.

   C. Ben had come to know his teacher very well and he would miss her when he moved next month.

   D. Ben had come to know his teacher very well; he would miss her when he moved next month.

9. DIRECTIONS: Choose the option that is NOT an acceptable correction to the sentence below.

   He knew that skipping school would be a problem, he did it anyway.

   A. He knew that skipping school would be a problem but he did it anyway.

   B. He knew that skipping school would be a problem, but he did it anyway.

   C. He knew that skipping school would be a problem, yet he did it anyway.

   D. He knew that skipping school would be a problem. He did it anyway.

DIRECTIONS: Choose the option that corrects an error in the underlined portion(s). If no error exists, choose "No change is necessary."

10. <u>A student</u> may not fully understand the amount of effort college requires; in fact, <u>many students</u> struggle because <u>he or she</u> don't allot enough time to complete all of the work.

   A. students

   B. a student

   C. they

   D. No change is necessary.

11. DIRECTIONS: Choose the sentence with correct parallel structure.

    A. My mother and I couldn't agree on anything: the movie we wanted to see, which restaurant to go to, or the day we wanted to meet.

    B. My mother and I couldn't agree on anything: the movie to see, the restaurant to go to, or the day to meet.

    C. My mother and I couldn't agree on anything: which movie to see, the type of restaurant we wanted, or the day we wanted to meet.

    D. My mother and I couldn't agree on anything: the movie to see, the restaurant we wanted to go to, or which day of the week to meet.

12. DIRECTIONS: Choose the sentence with no conventional errors.

    A. Karen had to act fast if she wanted to secure her dream job in California.

    B. Karen had to act fastly if she wanted to secure her dream job in California.

    C. Karen had to act quick if she wanted to secure her dream job in California.

    D. Karen had to act quickly if she wanted to secure her dream job in California.

DIRECTIONS: Read the passage, then answer the question below.

(1) The subject of whether or not Shakespeare should be studied in high school English classes has caused much debate. (2) On the one side, you have the diehard traditionalists who insist that learning to appreciate Shakespearean language is the crux of a well-rounded education. (3) However, others will argue that the archaic language used in Shakespeare's works is a source of confusion for students. (4) They also argue that today's students need more practice reading and interpreting the type of text they will be exposed to in a professional setting. (5) With valid arguments on both sides, this debate will most likely not be settled any time soon.

13. What is the best placement for the sentence below?

They also point out that because many modern-day sayings have roots in his works, studying Shakespeare will help students grasp the history of our language.

    A. after sentence 4

    B. after sentence 2

    C. after sentence 5

    D. after sentence 1

14. DIRECTIONS: Choose the sentence with no conventional errors.

    A. The teammates wore special uniforms in honor of their late coach.

    B. The teammates wore special uniforms in honor of its late coach.

    C. The teammates had worn special uniforms in honor of their late coach.

    D. The teammates have worn special uniforms in honor of its late coach.

15. Tina is interested in working as a teacher for an elite private school that rarely has openings. She wants to send her resume, so it is on file in the event a job does become available.

Which would be the best opening line for her cover letter?

    A. I understand that your institution rarely has openings, but I wanted to send you my impressive resume just in case something does pop up.

    B. While I know you generally only hire people who know current employees, I thought it wouldn't hurt to send my resume along.

    C. Please consider my extensive list of credentials as you conduct your end-of-year evaluations as I may be a good replacement for someone.

    D. Although I understand that there are no current openings, I would like you to have my resume on file in the event a position arises.

DIRECTIONS: Considering the context, choose the word that best completes the sentence below.

16. She was _____ for making unreasonable demands at every school board meeting.

    A. famous

    B. notorious

    C. accredited

    D. eminent

DIRECTIONS: Choose the option that corrects an error in the underlined portion(s). If no error exists, choose "No change is necessary."

17. The teacher was disappointed when her lesson on the <u>Holocaust</u> didn't have much of <u>an affect</u> on her students.

    A. holocaust

    B. a

    C. effect

    D. No change is necessary.

DIRECTIONS: Choose the option that corrects an error in the underlined portion(s). If no error exists, choose "No change is necessary."

18. Although she liked the temperate <u>weather</u> of Hawaii <u>better</u> <u>than</u> the humid weather in Florida, she moved to pursue her dream job at Disney World.

    A. whether

    B. best

    C. then

    D. No change is necessary.

DIRECTIONS: Choose the option that corrects an error in the underlined portion(s). If no error exists, choose "No change is necessary."

19. The man's <u>course</u> behavior <u>affected</u> his <u>whole</u> family.

    A. coarse

    B. effected

    C. hole

    D. No change is necessary.

DIRECTIONS: Read the following scenario, then answer the question that follows.

Marco is a college student interested in the treasurer position for the local chapter of the National Society of Collegiate Scholars. He needs to send an email to the president of the association detailing why he believes he is a good candidate for the position.

20. Which of the following statements fits the purpose, audience, and tone of the task?

    A. I am really into finances, am organized and detail-oriented, and prompt.

    B. My strong math, organizational, and time-management skills make me a good candidate for the position.

    C. While good math skills are a plus, I believe that my ability to socialize is what the association needs.

    D. Holding a leadership position looks good on a resume, so I would like to take on this challenge.

21. DIRECTIONS: Choose the sentence with correct parallel structure.

    a. No one in the office liked to deal with Mr. Williams because he was rude, talked too loudly, and demanded too much.

    b. No one in the office liked to deal with Mr. Williams because he was rude, loud, and demanded too much.

    c. No one in the office liked to deal with Mr. Williams because he spoke rudely and loudly, and was too demanding.

    d. No one in the office liked to deal with Mr. Williams because he was rude, loud, and demanding.

22. DIRECTIONS: Choose the sentence with no errors in structure.

    A. If only she had listened to her parents, she wouldn't be in this predicament.

    B. If she had only listened to her parents, she wouldn't be in this predicament.

    C. If she only had listened to her parents, she wouldn't be in this predicament.

23. DIRECTIONS: Choose the sentence that does **NOT** use the underlined word correctly.

    A. On the first day of class, the professor warned his students that they would need to take <u>copious</u> notes in class in order to earn a passing grade.

    B. The <u>unkempt</u> child was ostracized by her classmates.

    C. When she had to move, Lisa realized that she had accumulated a <u>verbose</u> amount of personal belongings.

    D. While he ignored his monthly credit card statement, the interest charges kept _.

DIRECTIONS: Read the passage, then answer questions 24-26. There are intentional errors included in the passage.

America Alligator Myths

(1) Many people buy into the many myths about the American Alligator without investigating the facts for themselves. (2) One of the more popular mistruths circulating is that if an alligator is chasing a person, he or she should run in a zigzag pattern. (3) Because alligators usually do not exceed 10-11 miles per hour or run for very long; someone can usually escape an alligator simply by running as quick as they can in the opposite direction. (4) Another common misconception is that alligators aren't good climbers when in fact, they have been seen climbing fences to escape captivity or get to water. (5) Installing a fence around the perimeter of a pool may not be sufficient to keep an alligator at bay. (6) Some erroneously believe that alligators live to be hundreds of years old. (7) They also believe that alligators can reach lengths of more than 20 feet and weigh thousands of pounds. (8) Although exact life expectancy ranges have not been established, most gators in the wild live no more than 50 years. (9) With so many rumors floating around, it is easy to see why the American alligator is so misunderstood.

24. Which sentence does **NOT** fit into the logical progression of the passage?

    a. sentence 7

    b. sentence 8

    c. sentence 3

    d. sentence 6

25. Which is **NOT** an acceptable edit for conventional errors in sentence 3?

    A. Because alligators usually do not exceed 10-11 miles per hour or run for very long, someone can usually escape an alligator simply by running as quickly as he or she can in the opposite direction.

    B. Someone can usually escape an alligator simply by running as quickly as he or she can in the opposite direction because alligators usually do not exceed 10-11 miles per hour or run for very long.

    C. Alligators usually do not exceed 10-11 miles per hour or run for very long; therefore, someone can usually escape and alligators simply by running as quickly as he or she can in the opposite direction.

    D. Because alligators usually do not exceed 10-11 miles per hour or run for very long: someone can usually escape an alligator if you run as quick as possible in the opposite direction.

26. Which sentence needs to be eliminated and why?

    A. Sentence 5 should be eliminated because it deviates from the topic.

    B. Sentence 7 should be eliminated because the information does not advance the previous idea.

    C. Sentence 10 should be eliminated because it repeats information presented in sentence 1.

    D. Sentence 7 should be eliminated because it deviates from the topic.

27. DIRECTIONS: Choose the sentence with no conventional errors.

    A. The class of 2016 presented it's gift to the principal at graduation.

    B. The class of 2016 presented its gift to the principal at graduation.

    C. The class of 2016 presented their gift to the principal at graduation.

28. DIRECTIONS: Choose the sentence with no conventional errors.

    A. When she decided which college she wanted to attend, her counselor squashed her dreams when she told her she did not have the minimum GPA or test scores to qualify for admission.

    B. When the student decided which college she wanted to attend, she squashed her dreams when she told her she did not have the minimum GPA or test scores to qualify for admission.

    C. When the student decided which college she wanted to attend, her counselor squashed her dreams when she told her she did not have the minimum GPA or test scores to qualify for admission.

29. DIRECTIONS: Choose the sentence with no conventional errors.

    A. He chose to not listen to his teacher during the lecture and therefore did not do well on the test.

    B. He chose not to listen to his teacher during the lecture and therefore did not do well on the test.

    C. He chose not listening over listening to his teacher during the lecture and therefore did not do well on the test.

30. DIRECTIONS: Choose the sentence with no conventional errors.

    A. When the dismissal bell rung, the doors flew open as the excited children ran outside.

    B. When the dismissal bell had rung, the doors flew open as the excited children ran outside.

    C. When the dismissal bell rang, the doors flew open as the excited children ran outside.

31. DIRECTIONS: Choose the sentence with correct modifier placement.

    A. Flying across the Gulf of Mexico, the man enjoyed the view from the window seat on the plane.

    B. Flying across the Gulf of Mexico, the man on the plane enjoyed the view from the window seat.

    C. As the plane flew across the Gulf of Mexico, he enjoyed the view from the window seat.

    D. As the plane flew across the Gulf of Mexico, the man enjoyed the view from the window seat on the plane.

DIRECTIONS: Considering the context, choose the word that best completes the sentence below.

32. The politician was _____, always looking for sneaky ways to slander his opponent.

    A. conscientious

    B. fastidious

    C. unscrupulous

    D. principled

33. DIRECTIONS: Choose the sentence that with no conventional errors.

    A. Lisa was overwhelmed by the copious amount of reading for the semester that included thousands of pages from her Women's Literature anthology, 20 chapters in her Macroeconomics textbook, and numerous online for Sociology 1102.

    B. Lisa was overwhelmed by the copious amount of reading for the semester: thousands of pages from her Women's Literature Anthology, 20 chapters in her macroeconomics textbook, and numerous online articles for Sociology 1102.

    C. Lisa was overwhelmed by the copious amount of reading for the semester: thousands of pages from her literature anthology, 20 chapters in her macroeconomics textbook, and numerous online articles for her sociology class.

34. DIRECTIONS: Correct the spelling error for the underlined word. Choice A shows the word as it appears in the sentence.

The toddler became inconsoleable when his mother left him with a babysitter.

    A. inconsaleable

    B. inconsolable

    C. unconsolable

    D. unconsoleable

35. DIRECTIONS: Choose the sentence with no conventional errors.

    A. One thing was clear: neither the administration nor the faculty was expecting the school grade to drop to an "F."

    B. One thing was clear: neither the administration nor the faculty were expecting the school grade to drop to an "F."

    C. One thing was clear: neither the administrators nor the teachers was expecting the school grade to drop to an "F."

36. DIRECTIONS: Choose the sentence with no conventional errors.

    A. When you order furniture online, one must often assemble it yourself.

    B. When I order furniture online, one must often assemble it myself.

    C. When one orders furniture online, you must often assemble it yourself.

    D. When you order furniture online, you must often assemble it yourself.

37. DIRECTIONS: Choose the sentence with no errors in structure.

    A. She was accustomed to a warm climate so she had no idea how to dress for the frigid weather.

    B. She was accustomed to a warm climate, having no idea how to dress for the frigid weather.

    C. She was accustomed to a warm climate, so she had no idea how to dress for the frigid weather.

    D. She had no idea how to dress for the frigid weather, because she was accustomed to a warm climate.

38. DIRECTIONS: Choose the sentence with no errors in structure.

    A. Although she didn't know how to drive one, riding on the back of the motorcycle, she enjoyed herself.

    B. Although she didn't know how to drive one, she enjoyed riding on the back of the motorcycle.

    C. Not knowing how to drive one, she enjoyed riding on the back of the motorcycle.

    D. Because she didn't know how to drive one, she enjoyed riding on the back of the motorcycle.

39. DIRECTIONS: Choose the option that corrects an error in the underlined portion(s). If no error exists, choose "No change is necessary."

When the plane finally landed on the runway after a long flight; the passengers elbowed each other in a mad rush to disembark.

    A. The plane finally landed on the runway after a long flight and the passengers elbowed each other in a mad rush to disembark.

    B. When the plane finally landed on the runway after a long flight. The passengers elbowed each other in a mad rush to disembark.

    C. The plane finally landed on the runway after a long flight, the passengers elbowed each other in a mad rush to disembark.

    D. When the plane finally landed on the runway after a long flight, the passengers elbowed each other in a mad rush to disembark.

40. DIRECTIONS: Choose the sentence that DOES contain a conventional error.

    A. She narrowed her prom dress choices down to two but couldn't decide if she liked the teal or the navy one better.

    B. She narrowed her prom dress choices down to two but couldn't decide if she liked the teal or the navy one best.

    C. She narrowed her prom dress choices down to two but couldn't decide between the teal dress or the navy dress.

41. DIRECTIONS: Choose the sentence that contains no conventional errors.

    A. Between my mom and my dad, I had to decide who I was going to take to the game.

    B. Between my mom and my dad, I had to decide which I was going to take to the game.

    C. Between my mom and my dad, I had to decide whom I was going to take to the game.

42. DIRECTIONS: Choose the option that corrects an error in the underlined portion(s). If no error exists, choose "No change is necessary."

I should of brought my umbrella to the party; there were torrential downpours all night.

    A. should have
    B. party,
    C. their
    D. No change necessary

1. C	9. A	17. C	25. D	33. C	41. C
2. B	10. C	18. D	26. B	34. B	42. A
3. C	11. B	19. A	27. B	35. A	
4. D	12. D	20. B	28. C	36. D	
5. A	13. B	21. D	29. B	37. C	
6. B	14. A	22. A	30. C	38. B	
7. C	15. D	23. C	31. D	39. D	
8. D	16. B	24. A	32. C	40. A	

1. **C.** Don't be fooled by choice B. It is missing the comma before the conjunction *and* that is necessary to properly join two independent clauses. Choice A is unclear. C is the most accurate way to communicate the thought.

2. **B.** *Inopportune* is the only choice that fits the context. *Ideal* and *auspicious* have positive connotations not fitting in the context of the rest of the sentence. Similarly, none of the meanings of *benign* (beneficial, gracious, kind, or favorable) work.

3. **C.** *Complement* means "to complete or make perfect." That is not the correct version to use in this sentence. *Compliment,* or "to praise" is the correct version of the homonym.

4. **D.** When dealing with a set number of items or things, *which* is the correct choice. When the number of things or items is not clear, use *what*. Also, when there are two items being compared, use *more*. *Most* is used for more than two items. Finally, the colon is used correctly in D. a semi colon would be incorrect.

5. **A.** Any word that is a language or a culture needs to be capitalized. Therefore, capitalize Cuban. In this case, the word *sandwich* does not because it is just a common noun.

6. **B.** This is the only choice that uses the correct verb tense.

7. **C.** To keep the verb tense consistent throughout the sentence, the past tense, *missed*, is the correct choice.

8. **D.** Use a semicolon to join two independent clauses that are related. Choice A is a comma splice; in choice B, the colon is used incorrectly; choice C is missing the comma needed before the conjunction to correctly join the independent clauses.

9. **A.** Tread carefully with the questions that have NOT or EXCEPT. It's a trap. Your brain will to a correct answer, but there are three correct ways to fix this sentence. You are looking for the incorrect fix, which is A since there is no comma before the conjunction, a requirement when joining two independent clauses.

10. **C.** This is testing your knowledge of pronoun-antecedent agreement. Since the second independent clause refers to *many students*, the proper pronoun is *they*, not *he or she*.

11. **B.** Look for parallel structure among the three things following the colon. All three in choice B start with a noun and are followed with a verb.

12. **D.** Adjectives and adverbs often get misused. Look at the word being complemented to figure these out. If it is describing a noun or pronoun, use an adjective. If it is modifying a verb, adjective, or another adverb, use an adverb. Since *quickly* is describing how Karen had to act, the adverb form is correct. Choice C is an adjective (quick). Even though choice A uses an adverb (fast), *quickly* is the preferred when using proper grammar. *Fastly* (B) is not a word.

13. **B.** This sentence is best after the second sentence because it elaborates on the arguments of diehard traditionalists. It doesn't make sense after sentence 1 (D) because it is not clear who *they* is referring to. It also doesn't work after sentence 4 (A) because that is discussing how the opposing side feels. Finally, it absolutely doesn't work after sentence 5, a clear conclusion to the paragraph.

14. **A.** Because the word *teammates* refers to the individual people on the team, *their* is the proper pronoun to use. Had it been the collective noun, *team*, the pronoun *its* would be correct. Remember collective nouns such as *team, class, faculty, board, band,* etc. are considered entities or things, not people. Even though these nouns are made up of individual people, they act as one unit.

15. **D.** Avoid sounding pretentious (choice C) or too casual (choices A & B). D is professional.

16. **B.** *Notorious* is being well known for something undesirable. This is the only work that fits the context of the sentence. Use the clues *unreasonable* and *demands* to match the tone.

17. **C.** *Affect/effect* are often confused. *Effect* is a noun in most instances while *affect* is a verb. Use the article *an* as a clue that a noun will follow. Other articles include *the* and *a*.

18. **D.** All of the underlined portions are correct as is.

19. **A.** When referring to someone's rude or rough, behavior, coarse is the correct word. Course refers to classes or a path.

20. **B.** This choice is professional and spells out relevant skills for the position.

21. **D.** Parallel structure is a must for clear communication. D is the only choice that uses adjectives throughout when describing Mr. Williams.

22. **A.** These types of questions are tricky! They all seem to be grammatically correct, but look closely at the usage. B implies that she listened to no one else except for her parents, so eliminate that choice. The syntax in C is not correct. A is the best choice because *only* is placed correctly.

23. **C.** This vocabulary question asks you to evaluate 4 words in context to determine which one is NOT used correctly. Using the process of elimination is the best bet for these, but remember, you are eliminating the choices that are used correctly. *Verbose* is not the correct word in context of the sentence in choice C because it has to do with wordiness, not physical objects.

24. **A.** Sentence 7, although still about alligators, interrupts the discussion about how long gators live and is not developed.

25. **D.** This is a NOT question. The use of a colon to join a dependent and independent clause is grammatically incorrect.

26. **B.** See explanation for #24.

27. **B.** The class is a collective noun; therefore, the possessive pronoun *its* is the correct choice. Remember to ignore the prepositional phrase when evaluating pronoun/antecedent agreement (and subject/verb agreement).

28. **C.** This is the only choice that clearly identifies who is going to college and who is squashing the dreams.

29. **B.** Don't split verb phrases, in this case *to listen* is the verb *phrase*. Keep the *to listen* together in the sentence. Keep the *not* before *to listen*. C is too wordy to be correct.

30. **C.** Make sure the verb tense stays consistent throughout the sentence. C is the only choice that accomplishes this (rang/flew).

31. **D.** This choice clearly identifies what flew and who enjoyed the view. A & B imply that the man was flying across the Gulf on his own, and C lacks an antecedent for the pronoun *he*.

32. **C.** Having scruples means having a strict moral code. Someone who is unscrupulous would be sneaky and slanderous. Context clues are vital for working these type of vocabulary questions out!

33. **C.** Course titles and book titles must be capitalized; general names of classes do not. C is the only choice that handles this properly. In A & B, the anthology is not a title, just the type of anthology (women's literature). In A, macroeconomics does not need to be capitalized.

34. **B.** Remember the "drop e" rule when adding suffixes that begin with a vowel. *Unconsolable* (C) is not a word.

35. **A.** Treat subjects that are separated by *neither/nor* or *either/or* as singular subjects. In this case, *administration* and *faculty* are collective nouns and therefore act as a single unit: *The administration was expecting… The faculty was expecting…*

36. **D.** Make sure to avoid pronoun shifts. Stick with the same voice (1st, 2nd, or 3rd person).

37. **C.** The rule is when joining two independent clauses, use a conjunction with a comma, eliminating A. B doesn't clearly communicate why she didn't know how to dress for frigid weather. In choice D, a comma is not necessary when adding a dependent clause to an independent clause.

38. **B.** This is the only choice that clearly identifies the relationship between the two clauses.

39. **D.** This choice is the best and most grammatically correct way to join a dependent clause with an independent clause. A is a run-on sentence. B erroneously places a period at the end of a dependent clause. C. is a comma splice.

40. **A.** Eliminate C because it is a run-on sentence. A is correct because the girl was choosing between two dresses. Best is used for more than two items.

41. **C.** *Who* is used for subjects; *whom* is used for objects. Ignoring the dependent clause, *Between my mom and my dad*, the subject of the independent clause, *I had to decide whom I was going to take to the game,* is *I. Whom* (mom or dad) is the object. Hint: When you can answer with *him* or *her*, use whom. Example: The answer to the question, *Who is she going to take?* would be *him* or *her*, not *he* or *she*.

42. **A.** Should *of* is NEVER correct. It is always should *have*.

GKT READING

1. **Knowledge of key ideas and details based on text selections**

- Identify textual evidence to support conclusions drawn from text.

- Identify explicit meaning and details within text.

- Determine inferences and conclusions based on textual evidence.

- Discriminate among inferences, conclusions, and assumptions based on textual evidence.

- Determine and analyze the development of central ideas or themes from one or more texts.

- Summarize one or more texts using key supporting ideas and details.

- Determine how and why specific individuals, events, and ideas develop based on textual evidence.

- Determine the cause and effect relationship(s) among individuals, events, and ideas based on textual evidence.

2. **Knowledge of craft and structure based on text selections**

- Interpret the meaning of words and phrases as used in text (e.g., figurative language, connotative language, technical meanings).

- Analyze how specific word choices shape meaning or tone.

- Analyze how the author uses organization and text structure(s) to convey meaning.

- Contrast the point of view of two or more authors on the same topic by analyzing their claims, reasoning, and evidence.

- Analyze how point of view and purpose shape the content and style of text.

3. **Knowledge of the integration of information and ideas based on text selections**

- Evaluate and relate content presented in diverse formats.

- Evaluate specific claims in text based on relevancy, sufficiency, and validity or reasoning.

- Synthesize information from a range of texts to develop a coherent explanation of a process, phenomenon, concept, or theme.

- Analyze multiple texts to differentiate approaches authors take to develop similar themes (e.g., mode, author's craft, genre, point of view).

1. ***Timing is everything.*** You have 55 minutes to read 4–5 passages (usually 4 passages with 1–2 of those being paired passages) and answer 40 questions. The number of questions per passage varies, so you will not spend equal time on each one. A good rule of thumb when prepping and when taking the test is to spend 3 minutes quickly reading the passages to get the overall understanding of the text, then 1 minute per question. You will absolutely need to go back into the text as you attack the questions, so saving time for this is critical!

    Example:

Passage	Number of Questions	Time Required
Passage 1	15 Questions	18 Minutes
Passage 2	13 Questions	13 Minutes
Passage 3	11 Questions	11 Minutes
Passage 4	10 Questions	10 Minutes
	Total Time	**52 Minutes**

2. ***Track your reading.*** Use your finger right on the screen or use your cursor; either way is fine. What matters is that you are keeping your place and your pace while reading actively and quickly. Not only is this a great test day strategy, it is something you want to do every time you read to build your speed. If you are practicing with printed text, use a pencil or pen to mark your place. Move the pencil or pen faster than your normal reading pace. Just like training for a race, you must push yourself and practice daily to increase your reading speed and comprehension.

3. ***Use the notepad.*** As you read, jot down words and phrases that show an opinion or argument (look for *emotion words*) to help you establish the author's attitude and tone. Descriptive adjectives are another good thing to write down. Record any "a-ha" moments you have or things you think are important. On paired passages, take a few minutes to jot down the overall idea from passage A before reading passage B. Establish the relationship between the two as soon as you are finished reading passage. This will go a long way in helping you answer the questions.

4. ***Pay close attention to the question stems.*** There are important phrases to help you determine exactly what the question is assessing.

    Key ideas and details. "According to the passage," "According to the author," "Based on the selection," and items similarly worded are key ideas and details questions. That means you will find the answer in the text, but the answer choice will NOT be worded exactly as it appears in the text. Look for a re-wording of that detail. Sometimes, the test makers like to throw in an "EXCEPT" or "NOT" in these detail questions. Make sure you pay attention to that—it is easier to overlook than you think. Eliminate the three choices that are in the text to reveal the one that is NOT.

    On the flip side, when you see "infer," "implies," or "suggests," you will need to use those tone words and things the author hints at to draw a conclusion. The answer will NOT be a re-worded detail, so eliminate any of those choices. With these types of questions, you must be absolutely sure that the choice you make can be backed up with evidence from the text. It is not a wild guess, but rather a conjecture based on evidence and reasoning.

Any item that mentions "central idea" or "main idea" is looking for the big idea the author wants to communicate about the topic or subject. It is more detailed than just the topic alone, but also not just one detail from the text. Any answer choice that is ONE detail from the text cannot be correct. Think of central/main idea as an umbrella with the details from the text being the spokes that keep it open. The collection of details in the text led you to and support the main idea. Beware: not all central/main ideas are explicitly stated. You must tease some of them out and make inferences. ***Helpful hint: "Choose the best title for the passage" is another way to ask about central/main idea.***

You may also see stems that ask for the "primary purpose" of the passage. It may also be worded something like "The author wrote the passage primarily to…" Both options are asking you why the author wrote the text and what he or she hoped to accomplish. This is where knowing the text structure (compare/contrast, cause/ effect, problem/solution, and order/sequence) will help you. Also, check out those words you recorded. They may contain hints about whether the author is describing something, arguing a point, analyzing both sides of a controversy, etc.

When a question asks about the tone of the passage, it is asking about the author's attitude toward the subject, a person in the text, or the reader. Using that list of words you recorded will often reveal the tone. ***Helpful hint: "The author would most likely agree (or disagree) with…" is another way to ask about the author's attitude.***

When you see, "In this context _____most nearly means," you are dealing with a vocabulary term. However, sometimes all four answer choices are synonyms/close synonyms of the word. Therefore, it is imperative to go back to the place in the text where the word is located and see which choice best fits the context. If you are not sure, use the plug-in method by replacing the word with each choice to see which one best fits.

Any question that asks for relationships between sentences and the rest of the passage or two passages is asking you to evaluate and synthesize information to draw conclusions about a concept or theme. Again, a simple detail cannot be the correct answer. The thought process for these questions is way more involved.

5. ***Look for tricky phrasing and extreme words.*** There will often be one word or one phrase in the distractors (that is, incorrect choices) that do not match what the question is asking or that make them flat-out wrong. Be especially careful with two-part answers; BOTH parts must be 100% accurate for the answer to be correct. Also, watch for words like "never," "always," "solely," etc. These extremities are rarely true.

6. ***Ask for and USE earplugs or headphones!*** It is so important for you to be able to concentrate and ignore distractions in the room, such as the person next to you typing and people coming in and out of the testing room. Earplugs or headphones really help you keep your head in the game. Wear them when you are prepping too!

7. ***Practice daily!*** Reading daily is the best way to build your speed, accuracy, vocabulary, and comprehension of difficult text. We recommend at least 15 minutes a day.

PASSAGE 1 - A SCOURGE RETURNS: BLACK LUNG IN APPALACHIA

DIRECTIONS: Read the passage below and answer the questions that follow.

A Scourge Returns: Black Lung in Appalachia

Carrie Arnold

Reproduced with permission from Environmental Health Perspectives

Once a month, a group of men in t-shirts, jeans, and baseball caps gather around a long table at the New River Health Clinic. The clinic, a small, one-story yellow clapboard building, is located in the tiny town of Scarbro, nestled in the bituminous hills of southern West Virginia. The members of the Fayette County Black Lung Association greet each other by name while they pour bitter black coffee into small Styrofoam cups.

In the early 1970s, coal workers' pneumoconiosis, or black lung, affected around one-third of long-term underground miners. After new dust regulations took effect, rates of black lung plunged. Today, however, they are once again rising dramatically.

Amidst the chatter and the coffee are the coughs. Some of the men hack loudly, others more quietly. All of them have advanced black lung, a disease they acquired working in the local mines. Although roughly 22% of underground miners smoke,[1] compared with about 18% of U.S. adults in general,[2] none of these men do. They gather not just as a support group but also to help one another complete the stacks of paperwork necessary to apply for government-mandated benefits for black lung and navigate the tortuous appeals process.

Aside from the group's leader, a bespectacled septuagenarian named Joe Massie, all the other members are in their 50s or early 60s. That's relatively young for someone with advanced black lung, and other workers are getting sick even earlier. These miners, who have gotten so sick so fast, are on the forefront of a wave of new black lung cases that are sweeping through Appalachia.

Scientists first noticed a troubling trend in 2005, when national surveillance conducted by the National Institute for Occupational Safety and Health (NIOSH) identified regional clusters of rapidly progressing severe black lung cases, especially in Appalachia.[3] These concerns were confirmed in follow-up studies using a mobile medical unit providing outreach to coal mining areas,[4,5] with later research showing that West Virginia was hit particularly hard.[6] Between 2000 and 2012, the prevalence of the most severe form of black lung rose to levels not seen since the 1970s,[7] when modern dust laws were enacted.[8]

Scarier still, the new generation of black lung patients have disease that in many cases progresses far more rapidly than in previous generations. Today, advanced black lung can be acquired within as little as 7.5–10 years of beginning work, says Edward Petsonk, a pulmonologist at West Virginia University. But not all cases progress so quickly; thus, occupational health researchers fear that what they are seeing now is only the tip of the iceberg.

1. According to the passage, why do health researchers fear there are more black lung cases that have yet to be discovered?

    A. Miners are not seeking medical care.

    B. Black lung advances within 7.5-10 years.

    C. Some cases will progress more slowly.

    D. The average age for onset cases is decreasing.

2. It can be inferred from context that a septuagenarian is:

   A. younger than 50 years of age.
   B. older than 60 years of age.
   C. between 50 and 60 years of age.
   D. younger than 60 years of age.

3. It can be reasonably assumed that laws enacted in the 1970s:

   A. reduced the cases of the most severe form of black lung but did not eradicate the disease.
   B. increased the cases of the most severe form of black lung temporarily.
   C. had no effect on the number of cases of the most severe form of black lung.
   D. permanently eradicated the most severe form of black lung.

4. According to the passage, clusters of quick-progressing black lung cases:

   A. were first noticed by the National Institute for Occupational Safety and Health (NIOSH) in West Virginia, with later studies pinpointing Appalachia as a hard-hit area.
   B. went unnoticed for years by the National Institute for Occupational Safety and Health (NIOSH) in Appalachia and West Virginia.
   C. were quickly brought under control through government-mandated programs offered by the National Institute for Occupational Safety and Health (NIOSH).
   D. were first noticed by the National Institute for Occupational Safety and Health (NIOSH) in Appalachia, with later studies pinpointing West Virginia as a hard-hit area.

5. Which statement would the author most likely agree with?

    A. The increase in black lung cases is a national health crisis.
    B. Black lung cases are worse among those who smoke.
    C. It is concerning that many new cases of black lung advance rapidly.
    D. Stricter dust laws need to be adopted to decrease new cases of black lung.

6. As used in the context of the passage, tortuous most nearly means:

    A. laborious.
    B. meandering.
    C. sinuous.
    D. straightforward.

7. What is the purpose of the first paragraph of the passage?

    A. to introduce the negative effects of pneumoconiosis on coal miners
    B. to highlight the poverty-stricken area in southern West Virginia
    C. to entice new members to join the Fayette County Black Lung Association
    D. to emphasize the human side of a disturbing health trend in southern West Virginia

8. Which title would NOT be an acceptable replacement?

    A. Appalachian Coal Miners Afflicted by Resurgence of Black Lung
    B. Retired Coal Miners Gear Up for Class Action Law Suit
    C. Conversation, Coffee, and Coughs: The Plight of Appalachian Coal Miners
    D. New Wave of Pneumoconiosis Cases Sweeping Appalachia

9. According to the information in the passage, which statement is NOT accurate?

    A. The percentage of smokers is drastically higher among coal miners than the general public.
    B. Researchers are concerned that more cases of pneumoconiosis have not yet been diagnosed.
    C. The government provides benefits for coal miners suffering from black lung.
    D. Dust laws seemed to decrease the number of new black lung cases when instituted in the 1970s.

10. Which best expresses the author's attitude toward the plight of the Appalachian coal miners?

    A. anger
    B. bitterness
    C. concern
    D. apathy

1. **C.** When you see "according to the passage," you are dealing with a ***key ideas and details question***. The answer will be in the text, but may not be worded exactly as it appears in the text. Eliminate A because the passage does not say anything about miners not seeking medical care. **B** is incorrect because advanced lung disease can be acquired within 7.5 to 10 years after beginning work, but those cases are the ones that are identified. **D** is a true statement but has nothing to do with the health researcher's concern about the potential cases. **C** is the correct choice because the cases that progress more slowly are those that have not yet been discovered.

2. **B.** This is a ***craft and structure question*** focused on vocabulary in context. Use the contrast context clue, "aside from the group's leader," to make the inference that a septuagenarian is older than the other men in their 50's and 60's. Having knowledge of Latin roots helps here too. *Sept-* means *seven*, so a *sept*uagenarian is someone in his 70s. No other answer choice fits this criteria.

3. **A.** This ***inference question*** will not be stated directly in the text, but information in passage will lead you to a logical conclusion. In paragraph 2, it says "After new dust regulations took effect rates of black lung plunged. Today, however, they are once again rising dramatically." Paragraph 5 also states that "Between 2000 and 2012, the prevalence of the most severe form of black lung rose to levels not seen since the 1970s when modern dust laws were enacted." These two pieces of information tell you that the cases were reduced, but not eliminated altogether, as evidenced by the resurgence of cases, making **A** the correct choice. The other answer choices contradict this information.

4. **D.** This answer to this ***detail question*** can be found in paragraph 5. The NIOSH identified cases in Appalachia with later research pinpointing West Virginia as a hard-hit area. **A** states the opposite. **B** and **C** are not supported by the text.

5. **C.** The trick answer here is **D**. While it seems like a reasonable statement, the author does not assert that stricter dust laws should be enacted. **A** is not correct because the disease is not a national crisis; it seems to be a regional crisis in Appalachia. There is no evidence to support the connection between smoking and black lung, eliminating **B**. The author would agree with **C** because this is the focus of the passage; she is bringing attention to the issue as a concern that needs to be acknowledged.

6. **A.** Although *meandering* (**B**) and *sinuous* (**C**) are synonyms for *torturous*, they are not the correct use in this context. They both mean *winding*; therefore, neither can be correct. *Straightforward* (**D**) is an antonym for *tortuous*. This leaves *laborious*, which means *tedious and time-consuming*, as the best choice.

7. **D.** Watch out for ***author's purpose questions***. You need to make an inference regarding why the author chooses a certain word, phrase, sentence, paragraph, or structure of the whole passage. You may want to choose **A** because it includes the phrase *to introduce*. At no time in paragraph 1 does the author bring up the negative effects of the disease. Ditto for **B**. Although you may be aware that the area is poverty-stricken, that is not the purpose of the paragraph. **C** may tempt you. However, if you look closely, you will not find many words that are enticing, including the name of the association itself. **D** is the best choice because it sets the stage for the passage by describing the monthly scene that involves the members of the Fayette County Black Lung Association, men who are affected by the disease.

8. **B.** Although the "NOT" is in all caps, it is easy to miss while taking a timed test. Remember, you are looking for the incorrect title. This throws many test takers. **B** is correct because the passage does NOT mention that the men are filing a lawsuit. The other choices are acceptable substitutes for the original title, as they offer insight into the main idea of the passage.

9. **A.** Look for extreme words or phrases. **A** is not accurate because although the percentage underground miners who smoke is slightly higher than the national average, the percentage is not *drastically* higher. The other choices are supported by the text.

10. **C.** The author's attitude can be teased out by looking at the words and phrases used. This piece is straightforward and does not include the emotionally charged wording of an author who is angry (**A**) or bitter (**B**). The author does not demonstrate apathy (**D**) (*lack of interest or concern*) for the coal miners. If the author were apathetic, she would not have written this piece. The human element along with the statistics included show that the author sees this as a concern to be addressed and wants to bring it to the public's attention.

DIRECTIONS: *Read the passage below and answer the questions that follow.*

Adapted from **Noise and Body Fat: Uncovering New Connections**

Wendee Nicole

Reproduced with permission from Environmental Health Perspectives

Studies on environmental noise and human health have uncovered associations with cardiovascular disease and diabetes. New research is delving further into possible metabolic effects of noise—specifically a possible link to weight gain. Investigators report that exposure to traffic noise at home was associated with body composition outcomes such as larger waist circumference and higher body mass index (BMI).

The cross-sectional study used data from the Danish Diet, Cancer, and Health Cohort, assessing 52,456 Danes between the ages of 50 and 64. The study tracked each participant's residential address history for the previous 5 years. The authors used noise-mapping software to estimate exposures from road traffic, railways, and air traffic for each address based on the most noise-exposed façade of the home. Four measures of body composition were recorded for each participant—BMI, waist circumference, body fat mass index (BFMI), and lean body mass index (LBMI).

Residential exposure to traffic noise has been associated with measures of weight gain. The body's response to both stress and lack of sleep may help explain why.

After adjusting for potential confounding factors (socioeconomic status, age, sex, and exposure to railway and aircraft noise), the researchers found that all measures of adiposity were significantly associated with road traffic noise. Each 10-dB increase in average road traffic noise exposure over 5 years was associated with an average increase in waist circumference of 0.35 cm and an average increase in BMI of 0.18 points. BFMI and LBMI also showed small but statistically significant increases in association with greater road traffic noise exposure. Co-exposure to railway noise louder than 60 decibels appeared to heighten the associations with BMI, waist circumference, and BFMI.

"The linear association we observed was consistent throughout the exposure range," says lead author Jeppe Christensen, a PhD candidate in epidemiology with the Danish Cancer Society Research Center. This is in line with other studies of similar health effects.

The authors propose that noise may activate the hypothalamus–pituitary–adrenal axis and the sympathetic nervous system—the body's "fight or flight" response. Evidence for this mode of action from other studies includes increased levels of cortisol associated with exposure to louder road noise. Noise may also disturb sleep, which is associated with increased food intake possibly due to dysregulation of hunger-related hormones, including leptin and ghrelin. Epidemiological studies have also reported that lack of sleep in children and young adults is associated with a higher percentage of body fat and increased waist circumference. A major strength of the study was its sheer size, and according to Bente Oftedal, an epidemiologist at the Norwegian Institute of Public Health, the results and conclusions matched the rigor of the performed analyses. "The main weakness is the lack of data on noise-related individual characteristics, such as noise annoyance and noise sensitivity," she says. "Both characteristics may modify associations between traffic noise and health outcomes, representing vulnerable subpopulations to noise exposure." Oftedal was not involved with the study.

"This is one of only a handful of studies investigating the association between exposure to noise in the environment and metabolic effects," says Charlotta Eriksson, a researcher at the Karolinska Institute's Institute of Environmental Medicine in Stockholm, who led one of the first studies to link aircraft noise with obesity. "The study by Christensen therefore adds valuable knowledge into this field of research."

The estimated effects of noise are small, Eriksson adds, but she says this is to be expected because other risk factors, such as heredity and lifestyle factors, are much stronger predictors of obesity for the individual. "Nevertheless," she says, "since a large proportion of the population is exposed to road traffic noise, the public health impact may be substantial."

1. According to the passage, exposure to road traffic noise:

    A. is the strongest predictor of obesity in individuals.
    B. has not been associated with weight gain.
    C. may substantially impact public health.
    D. has been unequivocally linked to obesity.

2. The title suggests that:

    A. the association between obesity and noise is widely accepted.
    B. the scientific study of obesity and noise is a relatively novel concept.
    C. the author disagrees with the idea that noise can cause increased weight.
    D. the link between increased weight and noise is a long-standing concept.

3. According to the article, what is one issue with the study?

    A. the absence of data on noise annoyance and sensitivity
    B. the small number of studies conducted in the field
    C. the lack of linear association throughout the exposure range
    D. the number of subjects involved in the study

4. Which is NOT identified as a possible reason that noise exposure can affect weight?

    A. activation of "fight or flight" response
    B. disruption of hunger-related hormones
    C. increased levels of cortisol
    D. heightened risk for diabetes

5. Which title would be an appropriate substitute?

    A. Noise and Obesity: A Definitive Link Unveiled
    B. Lack of Sleep and Larger Waist Size
    C. Noise Exposure and Weight-Related Diseases
    D. Study Uncovers Link between Adiposity and Noise Exposure

6. Which is NOT a measure of adiposity in this study?

    A. waist circumference
    B. body fat mass index
    C. body weight
    D. lean body max index

7. As used in context, *dysregulation* most nearly means:

   A. impaired response.
   B. normal development.
   C. genetic transmission.
   D. congenital defect.

8. What is the main idea of the first paragraph?

   A. Decreased exposure to environmental noise will result in better overall health.
   B. There is a definitive link between environmental noise and increased weight.
   C. Exposure to environmental noise is being explored as a possible cause of weight gain.
   D. Cardiovascular disease and diabetes risks increase with exposure to environmental noise.

9. As used in context, the phrase *metabolic effects* are:

   A. repercussions of environmental factors that affect cardiovascular health.
   B. outcomes of exposure to environmental factors that affect the regulation of weight.
   C. results of increased exposure to environmental factors that affect overall health.
   D. consequences of increased exposure to environmental factors that affect mental health.

10. Which statement contradicts information presented in the passage?

    A. Heredity and lifestyle factors have a minor impact on obesity.
    B. Exposure to traffic noise may increase the risk for obesity.
    C. Noise exposure is just one risk factor for obesity.
    D. Noise pollution affects a large part of the population.

1. **C.** The correct choice is supported in the last paragraph. Because so many people are exposed to traffic noise, the link between traffic noise and obesity can affect a significant part of the population. The information in **A** contradicts information in the last paragraph: "heredity and lifestyle factors are stronger predictors of obesity for the individual." **B** contradicts the main point of the entire passage. **D** uses strong language (*unequivocally*) that eliminates it as the correct choice.

2. **B.** **A**, **C**, and **D** can be eliminated because they all contradict the wording of the title. **B** is the only choice that captures the idea that noise exposure is newly charted territory.

3. **A.** The quote from Bente Oftedal in paragraph 6 reveals that **A** is the correct choice. The other choices contradict information in the passage.

4. **D.** Although diabetes is mentioned in paragraph 1, it is a separate issue that has already been studied along with cardiovascular disease. Because it is often associated with obesity, background knowledge might lead you to choose the wrong answer. Remember to use the information in the passage only for these types of questions.

5. **D.** **A** uses language (*definitive*) that does not match the tone of the passage. The author uses terms such as *possible* and *may*. Definitive means *conclusive,* and the author definitely does not present the link between noise and weight gain as conclusive. **B** only addresses one point made in the passage; therefore, it would not make a good title. **C** is intended to throw you off with the term *weight-related diseases.* The article does not talk about the diseases associated with weight gain, just the link between noise exposure and increased obesity risk. **D** is the only choice that rewords the title but still keeps the original meaning and intent.

6. **C.** While background knowledge tells you that body weight is a measure of adiposity (obesity), the passage does not mention it as a measure used. Again, watch for this, and only use information in the passage.

7. **A.** Using knowledge of prefixes will help you here. It means *abnormal or impaired.* Think of other words you know that begin with this prefix (*dysfunctional*, for example). Knowing this will eliminate **B**. C and D both relate to something you are born with and can therefore be eliminated as well.

8. **C.** The first paragraph sets the stage for a research study on noise exposure and weight gain, making **C** the correct choice. **A** seems like a reasonable statement, but is not even a consideration because it has nothing to do with the first paragraph. **B** uses that word *definitive* again, and we know the link the study made is not that strong. **D** is inaccurate.

9. **B.** The first word of each choice is a synonym for *effect.* However, the qualifying information in the rest of the answer choices for **A**, **C**, and **D** is inaccurate. The passage refers to weight gain, making B the correct choice.

10. **A.** This is a ***key ideas and details question***; therefore, the answer can be located within the text. **A** contradicts information presented in the passage while the rest of the answer choices mirror information presented in the passage.

DIRECTIONS: Read the passage below and answer the questions that follow.

Rudy: Autobiography Reveals Real Story Behind the Legend

Many know the story of Rudy, the undersized legend whose fierce desire to play football for Notre Dame made him one of the school's most famous graduates in history. Rudy has the kind of tenacity you can't help but admire. That's the thing about underdogs, they never give up. Now that the 1993 movie "Rudy" from Tristar Productions has been immortalized on the shelf as a beloved classic, Daniel "Rudy" Ruettiger shares the real, no-holds-barred, story in his autobiography "Rudy: My Story."

If you think you know the man who sacked the quarterback in the last 27 seconds of the game as fans chanted his name, you likely only know the Hollywood sports icon. But the book shows the story behind the man — Ruettiger's childhood and his motivations, failures, and successes.

He was the oldest son of an oil refinery worker in a strapped family of 14 children. It wasn't the kind of childhood that encouraged ambitious goals, but Rudy's dreams rose out of his modest home on the outskirts of Chicago. Those dreams took him from the clutches of despair to the glory of being a Notre Dame walk-on. He was carried off the football field on the shoulders of his teammates. But it wasn't all easy living from there.

Although Ruettiger is an inspirational hero who showed us how pure integrity and perseverance always triumph, his autobiography goes behind the scenes to reveal a regular guy. Ruettiger now uses the mistakes he made and the lessons he learned to motivate audiences across the country as an inspirational speaker.

As one of the most popular speakers in the U.S., Ruettiger reminds us how humble fame is born out of dire conditions. Fans and Midwest locals know that talk of Notre Dame means talk of the legendary Rudy — one of the most illustrious universities in America still celebrates an average Joe from Joliet, Ill.

But anyone who reads "Rudy" the book will learn more than that. They'll learn of a little boy's growing love for the Fighting Irish as he watched them at night on TV.

"Growing up in the Midwest, you start hearing about this place called Notre Dame before you can talk. It's a Catholic thing. You weren't even sure what college really meant, but the idea of it, the myth of it, the legend loomed large: If you were Catholic, you automatically had this dream of Notre Dame planted in your head. And if you went to Notre Dame, you were somebody."

1. As used in paragraph 1, "tenacity" most nearly means:

    A. aggressiveness.
    B. perseverance.
    C. obstinacy.
    D. vehemence.

2. Which of the following statements most accurately sums up the passage?

    A. It is possible to overcome obstacles in order to realize a challenging goal.
    B. Failures are just as important as successes in escaping a dire situation.
    C. Sports provide a pathway for lower middle-class students to attend college.
    D. Success in life is dependent on meeting societal expectations and ideals.

3. It can be reasonably inferred that Rudy's motivation in penning an autobiography is to:

    A. reignite public excitement about his phenomenal success at Notre Dame.

    B. reflect on his journey from the dire conditions of his childhood to infamy.

    C. clear up the misconceptions that the movie "Rudy" perpetuates.

    D. relate that it is not just his triumphs that define him, but also his failures.

4. The tone of the passage suggests that the author:

    A. admires the real Daniel "Rudy" Ruettiger.

    B. prefers the movie over the autobiography.

    C. is disinterested in the story behind the real Rudy.

    D. has a stake in the success of the autobiography.

5. The purpose of this passage is most likely:

    A. to promote the sale of "Rudy: My Story."

    B. to provide a review of "Rudy: My Story."

    C. to compare the movie, "Rudy" to "Rudy: My Story."

    D. to introduce a new generation to the movie "Rudy."

6. As used in paragraph 3, the term "strapped" most nearly means:

    A. imprisoned.

    B. modest.

    C. desperate.

    D. impoverished.

7. The central idea of the first paragraph is:

    A. Daniel "Rudy" Ruettiger was considered an underdog.

    B. Daniel "Rudy" Ruettiger gained fame at Notre Dame.

    C. Daniel "Rudy" Ruettiger wrote his authentic life story.

    D. Daniel "Rudy" Ruettiger paints himself as a hero.

8. In paragraph 2, "icon" most nearly means:

    A. symbol.

    B. superstar.

    C. legend.

    D. archetype.

9. The statement, "pure integrity and perseverance always triumph" reveals that:

    A. the author believes that good always prevails.

    B. the author has a pessimistic outlook on life.

    C. the author believes that failure is not an option.

    D. the author has completely unrealistic expectations.

10. In this passage, the use of the term "clutches of despair" implies that:

    A. Rudy's childhood was fraught with danger.

    B. Rudy's childhood was full of tribulations.

    C. Rudy's parents did not encourage his dreams.

    D. Rudy's parents were cold and uncaring.

PASSAGE 3 - ANSWER KEY AND EXPLANATIONS

1. **B**. *Tenacity* means *persistence* and *determination*, and it is the best answer out of the four. *Aggressiveness* aligns with the word *hostile*. *Obstinacy* means *stubborn*. *Vehemence* is *a feeling of passion*.

2. **A**. This is the only answer that is about the main idea. All the rest are details.

3. **D**. The reader can infer this because of this line in the passage, "Ruettiger now uses the mistakes he made and the lessons he learned to motivate audiences across the country as an inspirational speaker."

4. **A**. The passage is about an autobiography, not the movie. Therefore, the reader can assume the author is interested in the real-life person. The other answer choices do not fit.

5. **B**. Overall, this is a quick review of the autobiography. There is no promotion of anything in the passage, just an explanation of the autobiography.

6. **D**. *Strapped* in this case means *poor*. Therefore, *impoverished* is the best answer.

7. **C**. The main theme in the story is that Rudy wrote an autobiography outlining his real life. The other answer choices are details, not main ideas.

8. **C**. *Icon* means *symbol*. Do not fall for that here. *Icon* can also mean *legend*, which is more appropriate for this passage and in the context it is used.

9. **A**. This is a positive message of triumph. The author is NOT pessimistic or unrealistic, so **B** and **D** are out. In addition, the author mentions how Rudy's failures were important to his success, which makes **C** incorrect.

10. **B**. The central theme of Rudy's story and the article is that Rudy overcame a tough childhood of poverty and failures. Those are all *tribulations*, which means a *cause of great trouble or despair*.

DIRECTIONS: Read the passage below and answer the questions that follow.

What Was Chautauqua?

Adapted from The University of Iowa article Traveling Culture: Circuit Chautauqua in the Twentieth Century

Most people living today have not seen a Chautauqua. Originating in New York City, the first Chautauqua was in 1875. The Chautauqua Movement sought to bring learning, culture, and later, entertainment to the small towns and villages of America during the late 19th and early 20th centuries.

Much like a traveling circus, the Chautauqua would travel from town to town bringing educational lectures to people of different towns. It was originally called the Chautauqua Sunday School Assembly. Over time, the range of subjects grew exponentially: Hebrew and Greek in 1875, English literature in 1876, and French and German in 1878.

In 1878, William Rainey Harper, a prominent educator of the day, developed a home study program known as the Literary and Scientific Circle for those who could not attend the summer sessions. Around 7,000 people took part in the first year.

Local reading groups formed in communities throughout the nation to discuss the leading issues of the day. Later, a formal correspondence school was established, which provided certification for those who completed the rigorous studies and passed examinations. At its zenith, the Chautauqua officials also operated a large publishing house and a theological school.

As the years passed, more emphasis was placed on singing groups, oompah bands, theatrical presentations, and magic lantern shows. The advent of the railroads and their cheap fares had made it possible for working-class families to attend the sessions. The Chautauqua gatherings became a blend of a county fair and revival meeting.

By the turn of the century, many communities had formed their own "chautauquas," unrelated to the New York institution, that paid lecturers and performers to participate in their local events.

Over time, attendance for the Chautauqua started to dwindle. Following World War I, the availability of automobiles, radio programming, and motion pictures eroded the Chautauqua Movement's appeal. Annual attendance had remained around 45,000 at the general assembly each year between 1924 and 1932, after which attendance fell of sharply due to the Great Depression. Television was a further challenge. Independent local activities died out, but the national organization has continued on a reduced scale to the present day.

1. Which of the following is an assumption the author makes in this passage?

   A. William Rainey Harper, a prominent educator of the day, developed a home study program known as the Literary and Scientific Circle.

   B. Most people living today have not seen a Chautauqua. Originating in New York City, the first Chautauqua was in 1875.

   C. Local reading groups formed in communities throughout the nation to discuss the leading issues of the day.

   D. By the turn of the century, many communities had formed their own "chautauquas," unrelated to the New York institution.

2. How is the passage organized?

    A. An institution in American history is described, and then the essay goes on to give examples and details of that institution.
    B. A claim is made, and the then the essay goes on to support that claim.
    C. A description is given, and then the essay goes on to reveal the institution being described.
    D. A controversy is introduced, and the rest of the essay goes on to outline the main points of both sides.

3. What reason does the author give for the erosion of the Chautauqua Movement`s appeal?

    A. There is too much emphasis was placed on singing groups.
    B. The advent of the railroads and their cheap fares mad travel easier.
    C. The availability of automobiles, radio programming, and motion pictures took people away from Chautauqua.
    D. Many communities had formed their own "chautauquas."

4. What is the author's tone in this passage?

    A. challenging
    B. cynical
    C. sarcastic
    D. neutral

5. What can be inferred about Chautauqua after reading the passage?

    A. The people who started the Chautauqua felt it would be beneficial to the country as a whole to travel from town to town educating the American people.
    B. The people who started the Chautauqua wanted to make lots of money, so they traveled from town to town collecting ticket sales.
    C. The people who started the Chautauqua wanted people in other towns to speak many languages.
    D. The people who started the Chautauqua quit the production after WWII.

6. Using information from this passage, what would be the best caption for this photo?

    A. Since the late 1800s, people have flocked to participate in the Chautauqua.

    B. Crowds dwindle at Chautauqua because of TV.

    C. Thinking the circus came to town, crowds flock under tents to receive an education.

    D. Chautauqua, no longer an American institution.

7. The word *exponentially* in the second paragraph means:

    A. rapidly.

    B. slowly.

    C. steadily.

    D. continuously.

8. What is the main idea of the passage?

    A. The Chautauqua consisted of local reading groups formed in communities throughout the nation to educate people.

    B. The Chautauqua was a traveling movement that brought education to Americans across the country.

    C. By the turn of the century, many communities had formed their own "chautauquas."

    D. The Chautauqua included a range of subjects: Hebrew, Greek, English literature, French, and German.

9. What can be inferred from this statement?

"The availability of automobiles, radio programming, and motion pictures eroded the Chautauqua Movement`s appeal."

    A. People decided to drive themselves to the Chautauqua rather than wait for the Chautauqua to come to their town.

    B. Those who worked on the Chautauqua Movement later went on to work in motion pictures.

    C. Radio programs became the new Chautauqua.

    D. People lost interest in attending the Chautauqua, opting to go to the movies or listen to the radio instead.

10. Based on the last paragraph, what can the reader assume?

    A. Television completely wiped out the Chautauqua.

    B. The Chautauqua is still a robust movement today.

    C. Although the Chautauqua is not as prominent today, some do still exist

    D. The Chautauqua can only be attended in New York City.

1. **B.** The author does not know that "most people living today have not seen a Chautauqua." We know the author assumes this because of other clues stated in the passage: (1) *Originating in New York City, the first Chautauqua, was in 1875*; (2) *Following World War I; the availability of automobiles, radio programming, and motion pictures eroded the Chautauqua Movement`s appeal*; and (3) *Annual attendance had remained around 45,000 at the general assembly each year between 1924 and 1932, after which attendance fell of sharply due to the Great Depression.*

2. **A.** The author discusses the institution of the Chautauqua, then goes on to explain the Chautauqua, and then gives specific examples: Hebrew and Greek in 1875, English literature in 1876, French and German in 1878; Local reading groups formed in communities throughout the nation to discuss the leading issues of the day; Chautauqua gatherings became a blend of a county fair and revival meeting.

3. **C.** The last paragraph of the passage states: "The availability of automobiles, radio programming, and motion pictures eroded the Chautauqua Movement`s appeal. Annual attendance had remained around 45,000 at the general assembly each year between 1924 and 1932, after which attendance fell of sharply due to the Great Depression. Television was a further challenge. Independent local activities died out, but the national organization has continued on a reduced scale to the present day."

4. **D.** This passage is strictly informational. The author does not take a position or try to persuade the reader. The author is simply talking about Chautauqua in an objective manner.

5. **A.** Chautauqua was an education movement. It can be inferred that planning and executing these huge events all over the country was probably motivated by people's desire to educate the country's people.

6. **A.** C is designed to distract you. Do not fall into the trap of looking at the tent, thinking *circus,* and recalling that a *traveling circus* was mentioned in the passage. The best answer is **A** because it best supports the photo and what is presented in the passage.

7. **A.** C and **D** are out because *continuously* and *steadily* are the same in this situation. We know *slowly* is not correct, so **A** is the best answer.

8. **B.** All the other answer choices are details from the passage, not main ideas.

9. **D.** The correct answer can be inferred based on this sentence in the last paragraph: *The availability of automobiles, radio programming, and motion pictures eroded the Chautauqua Movement`s appeal.*

10. **C.** We know Chautauqua still exists "on a reduced scale to the present day" as stated in the last paragraph. In addition, **A** uses strong language (*completely*). D also uses strong language (*only*). Stay away from strong language like *always, completely, never, zero*. These are called absolutes.

DIRECTIONS: Read the passage below and answer the questions that follow.

James Buchanan Eads and the St. Louis Bridge

When looking down on the Mississippi River from the top of the Gateway Arch, many visitors remark upon the graceful-looking bridge to the north. It is hard to imagine that this bridge is the product of immediate post-Civil War engineering, that it was the first bridge built with structural steel, or that 15 men died of a mysterious illness while constructing it. Even more amazing is the fact that it was designed by a man who never built a bridge before.

The designer was James Buchanan Eads, born in Lawrenceburg, Indiana, in 1820. Eads had very few years of early schooling due to his father's financial problems. In 1833, Eads arrived in St. Louis as a penniless 13-year-old boy who sold apples on the street. He soon obtained a position as a clerk with a merchant named Barrett Williams, who let the young Eads read extensively in his private library.

Later on, Eads decided to tackle a problem with steamboats and their frailties. In an era when boats were beset by many dangers, such as snags, sandbars, exploding boilers, and hot cinders, steamboats often sank, taking their cargo with them to the bottom of the river. Oftentimes, a good share of the cargo survived intact and could be recovered.

Businessmen were willing to pay a lot of money to get cargoes back. Eads designed a surface boat to salvage sunken ships and cargo. Eads' salvage company was soon the most successful on the river, and he made a fortune, retiring in 1857 at age 37.

At the conclusion of the Civil War, long-standing dreams of a bridge across the Mississippi River at St. Louis were revived. A bridge became a necessity by the late 1860s. The width of the river at St. Louis had created a problem with commercial transportation after the beginning of railroads. Without a bridge, freight could not be transported across the river. Instead cargo had to be off-loaded from trains to ferry boats. This increased the price of goods.

James B. Eads presented an innovative plan to build the bridge. The plan was approved in 1867. Although a rival, Lucius Boomer, still had the rights to build the bridge, he took no legal action against the Eads project. Boomer had already delayed construction long enough for four new bridges, built further upstream, to serve Chicago's railroads.

Eads' design was radical. The building material, steel, was new, as was his daring solution to the problems imposed upon him. The design of the bridge did not use the popular form of construction, the truss, or even the newer suspension system, but instead hearkened back to the ancient Roman arch for support. Each arch would consist of four ribs, arranged in parallel pairs, rising beneath a double deck roadway. Eads' plans were thought radical by some, mad by others. He had never built a bridge before, and even his supporters wanted him to consult an experienced bridge engineer. As the bridge neared completion, the people of St. Louis saw a graceful structure with three huge arches of steel, more than 500 feet long. The central arch spans 520 feet, the two side arches span 502 feet each. The upper deck was for carriages and horsemen; the lower deck was for the railroad. The bridge was "over-designed" by Eads to appear strong to the layman. The confidence of the public was important and would ensure that the bridge was used.

The great bridge at St. Louis was not the last of Eads' projects. He was later instrumental in building the first permanent mouth of the Mississippi into the Gulf of Mexico by using a system of jetties that guided sediment deposition.

1. What is the main idea of the passage?

   A. The design of the bridge did not use the popular form of construction, the truss, or even the newer suspension system.
   B. At the conclusion of the Civil War, long-standing dreams of a bridge across the Mississippi River at St. Louis were revived.
   C. James Buchanan Eads was a self-taught genius.
   D. Having little experience, James Buchanan Eads built an engineering marvel that helped connect two sides of the Mississippi.

2. The tone of this passage is?

   A. approving.
   B. cynical.
   C. indignant.
   D. endearing.

3. What was different about this bridge from other bridges built before?

   A. This bridge would be much bigger.
   B. The design of the bridge did not use the popular form of construction.
   C. The building material used was cement instead of steel.
   D. The bridge was built by using boats.

4. According to paragraph 6, what can be inferred regarding why Boomer's company did not take legal action against Eads?

   A. Boomer's company was already too busy with work from other delayed projects, and seeking legal action would put them farther behind.
   B. Boomer was afraid to take legal action against Eads because Eads was radical in his thinking.
   C. Eads would have counter-sued Boomer's company for stalling the construction.
   D. At the conclusion of the Civil War, people wanted the bridge, and Boomer did not want to disappoint them.

5. Why does the author include Eads' lack of formal education in the first paragraph?

   A. To commend Barrett Williams, who let the young Eads read extensively in his private library.
   B. To show that despite Eads' lack of education, he was still able to build one of the biggest engineering marvels of the 20th century.
   C. To criticize Eads' father for not taking better care of his son's education.
   D. To showcase a time in American history when education was not the central focus.

6. Why does the author include Eads' endeavors salvaging sunken boats?

   A. To compare and contrast Eads' and Boomer's companies.
   B. To show that Eads' had the most successful salvage company.
   C. To show that Eads' always had a knack for doing the unexpected in unconventional ways.
   D. To showcase Eads' business skills and savviness.

7. Which of the following statements about the bridge's design is NOT supported by the passage?

    A The design of the bridge did not use the popular form of construction.

    B. The central arch spans 520 feet, the two side arches span 502 feet each.

    C. The upper deck was for carriages and horsemen; the lower deck was for the railroad.

    D. The bridge's arches were built for aesthetic purposes, not for structural support.

8. As used in the passage, the following statement:

"Eads' salvage company was soon the most successful on the river, and he made a fortune, retiring in 1857 at age 37."

    A Provides background knowledge about Eads that is not relevant to the rest of the story and should be deleted.

    B. Provides background knowledge about Eads that helps explain his determination to face challenging tasks.

    C. Shows Eads is the best bridge builder of all time.

    D. Shows Eads to be cunning and conniving, which he applied when he took Boomer's contract for the St. Louis bridge.

9. Using the information from the passage, please choose the best caption for the photo below:

    A Many cross the new St. Louis Bridge, Eads' engineering feat.

    B. Construction stalled as Eads and Boomer fight over bridge contract.

    C. Crossing the Mississippi on the first of its kind.

    D. Skeptical at first, St. Louis tourists cross the Mississippi on Eads Bridge.

10. This passage would most likely appear in a(n):

        A. editorial critiquing Eads as a businessperson.

        B. newspaper advertising for bridge workers.

        C. social studies textbook on American innovation.

        D. literature book of stories of bridges.

1. **D. D** is the best answer because it encompasses the entire passage. **A** and **B** are details from the passage but not a main idea. **C** is too extreme; the word *genius* is never used or implied.

2. **A.** The person writing this passage obviously likes Eads and thinks he was an important figure in American innovation. Therefore, the passage is *approving*. *Cynical* means *distrustful*. *Indignant* means *anger or annoyance at unfair treatment*. *Endearing* is *inspiring love or affection*, which is too sentimental for this passage.

3. **B.** This sentence from the passage explains why **B** is the best answer: "The design of the bridge did not use the popular form of construction, the truss, or even the newer suspension system, but instead hearkened back to the ancient Roman arch for support."

4. **A.** This sentence from the passage explains why **A** is the answer: "Although a rival Lucius Boomer still had the rights to build the bridge, he took no legal action against the Eads project. Boomer had already delayed construction long enough for four new bridges, built further upstream, to serve Chicago's railroads."

5. **B.** Although Barrett Williams did allow Eads to read in his private library, **A** is not the correct answer. The fact that Eads was not formally educated adds to the fact that he was able to build such an amazing and important bridge. **C** and **D** were never mentioned in the passage.

6. **C.** Using the sunken boats as a way to show his problem-solving skills and perseverance was a way for the author to show Eads as an unconventional thinker.

7. **D.** *Aesthetic* means *beauty*. While the arches were pretty, that was not their purpose. They were made for structural support too, as seen in this sentence: "The design of the bridge did not use the popular form of construction, the truss, or even the newer suspension system, but instead hearkened back to the ancient Roman arch for support. Each arch would consist of four ribs, arranged in parallel pairs, rising beneath a double deck roadway."

8. **B.** The sentence from the passage implies that Eads defies odds and is able to accomplish great things, which is relevant to the passage.

9. **A.** Remember, the passage is about Eads, so his name should be in the caption. **A** is the best choice of the four choices.

10. **C.** The entire passage is about Eads and his innovative ways. The passage does not critique or advertise anything. This is informational text, not literature.

PASSAGE 6 – ALTERNATIVE EDUCATION

DIRECTIONS: Read the passages and answer the questions that follow.

Passage A

The past 18 months shook up state education communities preparing students to earn a high school equivalency certificate. With some states dropping the old test for new ones, states choosing to have multiple options, and the implementation of College and Career Ready (CCR) standards, the landscape drastically changed in a short period of time.

Here is what educators and those looking to achieve this educational milestone should know about the past year and a half:

1. 2014 marked the first year in U.S. history that alternative tests were used by states. Twenty states administered alternative tests after choosing to either drop the GED test within their state or offer multiple tests for students to choose from. The HiSET exam developed by Educational Testing Service and the TASC Test Assessing Secondary Completion by CTB/McGraw Hill allow those who have not completed high school the opportunity to earn their high school equivalencies. Introducing numerous branded tests broke conventional terms and understanding of how people actually go about earning a high school credential.

2. People are learning you don't "get a GED." Employers, education administrations, and institutions of higher education incorrectly ask whether an applicant has his or her "GED." Having proof of a high school credential is essential for many careers and postsecondary education opportunities. However, the GED is a test, not something earned. HiSET, GED, and TASC scores are mobile, meaning they can be used for employment and college applications throughout the United States. Test takers now have a choice as to what test they choose to take based on various categories such as price or whether the test is available in paper and/or computer-delivered formats.

3. The results are the same. All three tests measure high school equivalency skills, and each has implemented CCR standards. Whether one takes the HiSET, GED, or TASC test, the end result when passing these tests is the individual earning a state-issued credential. For example, in California, a student can take either test and earn the California High School Equivalency Certificate when passing each test's subject areas.

The trend toward alternative testing shows no signs of slowing as more states consider new test options and vendors in the near future. Options in how one earns a high school credential have changed, but the outcomes are the same — increasing one's ability to achieve a more secure future by reaching this education milestone.

Passage B

Impeccably green mountains overlook a picturesque New England landscape as families gaze upon capped and gowned graduates sitting along mahogany benches. One cannot help but think of this scene as suited only for institutions of the academic elite.

However, a different educational success occurs in this part of New Hampshire, where students wear jumpsuits and study in cells.

Grafton County Department of Corrections in North Haverhill, 35 miles north of Dartmouth College, prides itself on the number of inmates it's able to graduate from the state's new high school equivalency test called HiSET.

"We're the HiSET jail; we get inmates an education," said correctional educator Kenn Stransky.

A teacher for the last 15 years, 8 at the facility, Stransky has led numerous initiatives borrowed from more conventional education environments. For Stransky, to have a real impact on these students, it's about creating an education-focused culture.

"A student is a student," says Stransky on how he views this unique student population. One such initiative is an alumni tutoring program, in which inmates who've earned their high school equivalency certificate help current inmates who are preparing to take the tests.

"I'm here only once a week, so that's a limited opportunity, but their inmate peers are here all the time and can provide continuous support," Stransky said.

Support for education success goes beyond those directly involved with the education program. Down to each correctional officer, everyone shares the responsibility to motivate inmates to enroll voluntarily and earn their high school equivalency.

"We want them to be a more prepared and better people when they leave the facility," program officer Sgt. Mark Deem said. "Confidence that they could achieve something really makes a difference on whether we'll see them again."

Inmates tend to gain a sense of purpose by graduating from the program, which has been shown to reduce recidivism.

Inmates who participated in education programs have a 43 percent lower chance of recidivating than those who did not, according to a 2013 RAND Corporation study funded by the U.S. Departments of Education and Justice.

The facility's honor graduate during this recent graduation is 45-year-old Mary Howard. Howard said that coming from a broken home, hanging around with the wrong crowd, and illegal substance use led her to drop out of school early. However, the support and encouragement she received from fellow inmates and the facility's staff kept her focused and driven.

"I have a completely different outlook on my future because there are more opportunities for me when I get out," Howard said.

1. According to Passage 1, what common misconception surrounds the GED?

    A. that employers do not recognize it
    B. that it is earned through a program
    C. that it is being phased out
    D. that there are many test options

2. Which quote from Passage 2 illustrates how the Grafton County Department of Corrections is helping inmates prepare for the types of tests addressed in Passage 1?

    A. "One such initiative is an alumni tutoring program, in which inmates who've earned their high school equivalency certificate help current inmates who are preparing to take the tests."

    B. "Inmates tend to gain a sense of purpose by graduating from the program, which has been shown to reduce recidivism."

    C. "A teacher for the last 15 years, 8 at the facility, Stransky has led numerous initiatives borrowed from more conventional education environments."

    D. "Grafton County Department of Corrections in North Haverhill, 35 miles north of Dartmouth College, prides itself on the number of inmates it's able to graduate from the state's new high school equivalency test called HiSET."

3. Which technique does the author employ for the first paragraph of Passage 2?

    A. engage in storytelling

    B. use surprising statistics

    C. report background information

    D. provide a detailed description

4. As used in Passage 2, what does "recidivism" most closely mean?

    A. rehabilitation

    B. remorsefulness

    C. relapse

    D. respite

5. Identify the main idea of Passage 1 in relation to the main idea of Passage 2?

    A. Passage 1 discusses changes to the options for high school equivalency testing, while Passage 2 highlights a program that utilizes one of the high school equivalency assessments.

    B. Passage 1 argues for tougher high school equivalency requirements, while Passage 2 tells the story of a former inmate who is successful because he earned his high school credentials via the HiSET.

    C. Passage 1 criticizes the alternative testing options for high school equivalency, while Passage 2 praises the HiSET as an assessment that provides opportunity for juvenile inmates.

    D. Passage 1 asserts that without a high school diploma or its equivalent, there are no opportunities for the future, while Passage 2 claims that all students, even those in jail, deserve an education.

6. According to Passage 2, what makes the Grafton County Department of Corrections high school equivalency program successful?

    A. the picturesque setting of the correctional facility

    B. the support and encouragement of fellow inmates and staff

    C. the implementation of a strict study schedule

    D. the conventional educational environment

7. According to Passage 1, the HiSET, GED and TASC:

    A. require courses to demonstrate test-readiness.
    B. are tailored to specific state standards.
    C. follow the guidelines of the CCR standards.
    D. measure completely different outcomes.

8. What assertion does the author make in the concluding paragraph of Passage 1?

    A. that options for a successful future hinge upon earning a high school diploma or its equivalency
    B. that assessment companies can expect to earn record-breaking profits as more people choose to test
    C. that credentials for earning a high school diploma will remain relatively unchanged in the near future
    D. that it has become increasingly difficult for students to demonstrate mastery of the new CCR standards

9. What do the last paragraph of Passage 1 and the last paragraph of Passage 2 have in common?

    A. They both offer proof of the current trend of students choosing alternative routes to earning a high school education.
    B. They both detail the various options available to nontraditional students for earning a high school education.
    C. They both provide details to show that although there are alternatives, a traditional high school education is preferable.
    D. They both have an optimistic view on the opportunities that are afforded by earning high school credentials.

10. As used in Passage 1, *credential* most nearly means:

    A. identity.
    B. qualification.
    C. documentation.
    D. passport.

1. **B**. The answer is embedded in the second bullet in this passage. "However, the GED is a test—not something earned." Information in bullet 2 also eliminates **A** as a choice. Information in the last paragraph contradicts **C**. Finally, while there are several test options, **D** does not answer the question. Avoid this trap.

2. **A**. Tread carefully on these types of questions. All four quotes are taken directly from the text, and your task is to identify the one that *best* answers and provides evidence for the question. While all choices address the benefits of the program, only **A** addresses the support inmates are given while preparing for the test.

3. **D**. The imagery used in paragraph 1 provides a detailed description, making **D** correct. The author does not engage in storytelling (**A**) or provide any statistics (**B**). The tone is not a simple, objective report, eliminating **C**.

4. **C**. Use the plug-in method. *Rehabilitation* is the goal; therefore, it would not be desirable to reduce it, making **A** incorrect. Ditto for *remorsefulness* (**B**). *Respite* means *rest*, and that does not make sense in the context of the sentence, thus eliminating **D**. *Relapse* (**C**) is the only choice that fits.

5. **A**. On these types of questions, you need to make sure both parts of the answer are correct. **A** is the only answer that fits this criteria. **B** gives incorrect information about both passages. **C** gives incorrect information for Passage 1. **D** uses the absolute trick for the first part of the answer: *"...there are no opportunities for the future..."*

6. **B**. While the picturesque setting is nice (**A**), it has no bearing on the success of the program. A strict study schedule is not mentioned, making **C** incorrect. Eliminate **D** because this program is unconventional, not conventional. **B** is reiterated throughout the text, making it the best choice.

7. **C**. The answer is embedded in the third bullet. **A** can be eliminated because no programs are *required* before taking these tests. Because the standards are Common Core, they are not specific to the states, making **B** incorrect. **D** is contradicted by information in the text (see bullet 3).

8. **A**. Only **A** is supported by information in the passage. Information in the paragraph contradicts **C**. **B** and **D** are not supported by anything in the last paragraph or the passage in general.

9. **D**. When analyzing the answer stems for **A**, **B**, and **C**, you see terms such as *detail* and *proof*. The last paragraph of each passage does not provide details and proof, but they both offer an optimistic outlook for these diploma options, making **D** correct.

10. **B**. This is an example of the answers all being synonyms for the target word. Plug in the choices to see which one fits best into the context of the sentence, paragraph, and passage. *Qualification* (**B**) is the only one that fits in context of the passage and the two sentences where the word is used (see bullet 3 and last paragraph).

GKT MATH

I. **Knowledge of number sense, concepts, and operations**

- Compare real numbers and identify their location on a number line.

- Solve real-world problems involving the four operations with rational numbers.

- Evaluate expressions involving order of operations.

II. **Knowledge of geometry and measurement**

- Identify and classify simple two- and three-dimensional figures according to their mathematical properties.

- Solve problems involving ratio and proportion (e.g., scaled drawings, models, real-world scenarios).

- Determine an appropriate measurement unit and form (e.g., scientific notation) for real-world problems involving length, area, volume, or mass.

- Solve real-world measurement problems including fundamental units (e.g., length, mass, time), derived units (e.g., miles per hour, dollars per gallon), and unit conversions.

III. **Knowledge of algebraic thinking and the coordinate plane**

- Determine whether two algebraic expressions are equivalent by applying properties of operations or equality.

- Identify an algebraic expression, equation, or inequality that models a real-world situation.

- Solve equations and inequalities (e.g., linear, quadratic) graphically or algebraically.

- Determine and solve equations or inequalities, graphically or algebraically, in real-world problems.

- Graph and interpret a linear equation in real-world problems (e.g., use data to plot points, explain slope and y-intercept, determine additional solutions).

- Identify relations that satisfy the definition of a function.

- Compare the slopes of two linear functions represented algebraically and graphically.

IV. **Knowledge of probability, statistics, and data interpretation**

- Analyze data presented in various forms (e.g., histograms, bar graphs, circle graphs, pictographs, line plots, tables) to solve problems.

- Analyze and evaluate how the presentation of data can lead to different or inappropriate interpretations in the context of a real-world situation.

- Calculate range, mean, median, and mode of data sets.

- Interpret the meaning of measures of central tendency (i.e., mean, median, mode) and dispersion (i.e., range, standard deviation) in the context of a real-world situation.

- Analyze and evaluate how the selection of statistics (e.g., mean, median, mode) can lead to different or inappropriate interpretations in the context of a real-world situation.

- Solve and interpret real-world problems involving probability using counting procedures, tables, and tree diagrams.

- Infer and analyze conclusions from sample surveys, experiments, and observational studies.

NUMBER SENSE

When comparing numbers, especially decimals and negative numbers, a number line can be used to help visualize the values of the numbers. The first step in solving these problems should be to convert all numbers to decimals. Find the whole number values the decimals fall in between. Place the decimals on the number line. Remember, the greatest value is always the number furthest right.

Example 1:

Which number is greater, $-\frac{9}{5}$ or $-\frac{11}{6}$?

Step 1- Convert both to decimals. Now we are comparing -1.8 and -1.83.

Step 2- Both of these numbers fall between -1 and -2 on the number line. Set up your number line.

-1.83 is closer to -2, so when inserted on the number line,

you can see that -1.8, or $-\frac{9}{5}$ is the greater number.

ORDER OF OPERATIONS

"Please Excuse My Dear Aunt Sally"

P – Parenthesis or any other grouping (brackets, absolute value)

E – Exponents

MD – Multiplication/Division- **whichever comes first when reading left to right

AS – Addition/Subtraction- **whichever comes first when reading left to right

*Keep your work organized by underlining the step you are completing in each step.

Example 1:

Evaluate:

$$9(3 + 2) - 15 \div 3$$

Following order of operations:

$$9(5) - 15 \div 3$$
$$45 - 5$$

The answer is 40.

Example 2:

Evaluate:

$$10 \div 5 \times 6^2 + |2 - 8|$$

Following order of operations:

$$10 \div 5 \times 6^2 + |-6|$$
$$10 \div 5 \times 6^2 + 6$$
$$10 \div 5 \times 36 + 6$$
$$2 \times 36 + 6$$
$$72 + 6$$

The answer is 78.

PROPORTIONS

Whenever you are given a ratio or an equivalence statement (ex. On a map, 1 inch represents 35 miles), you can set up a proportion. You can also think of it as you are being given three of four things needed. You must find the fourth by using the proportion. When setting up proportions, we tell our students to think *matchy matchy*, whatever you put on the top of the proportion must be the same or match the other side of the proportion. For example, $\frac{dollars}{units} = \frac{dollars}{units}$ or $\frac{units}{dollars} = \frac{units}{dollars}$. Both are correct because they match. Give yourself a key to make sure you are setting it up correctly. Once your proportion is set up, you can cross multiply to find the missing value.

Example 1:

A worker can assemble 5 computers every 3 hours. At this rate, how many computers can be assembled in 10 hours?

To solve, give yourself a key and plug in what you know:

$$\frac{computers}{hours} \qquad \frac{5}{3} = \frac{x}{10}$$

Next, cross multiply to get

$$5(10) = 3x$$

Solve for x:

$$50 = 3x$$

$$x = \frac{50}{3} \ or \ 16.67 \ computers$$

Example 2:

If 4 pounds of candy costs $3.75, how much will 7 pounds cost?

To solve, give yourself a key and plug in what you know:

$$\frac{pounds}{\$\$} \qquad \frac{4}{3.75} = \frac{7}{x}$$

Next, cross multiply to get

$$7(3.75) = 4x$$

Solve for x:

$$26.25 = 4x$$

$$x = \frac{26.25}{4} \ or \ \$6.56$$

SLOPE

Slope is represented by "m" in slope intercept form ($y = mx + b$), "rise over run", or $\frac{\Delta y}{\Delta x}$. The formula often used is: $\frac{y_1 - y_2}{x_1 - x_2}$

The clue words for finding slope are "parallel" and "perpendicular."

Parallel lines: Parallel lines have the exact SAME SLOPE. Parallel lines will never intersect. Ex: $y = \frac{1}{2}x + 2$ and $y = \frac{1}{2}x - 3$

Perpendicular lines: Perpendicular lines have OPPOSITE RECIPROCAL slopes. This means that one will be positive, one will be negative, and their slopes will be "flipped."

Ex: $y = \frac{4}{3}x + 1$ and $y = -\frac{3}{4}x + 5$.

There are two ways which you may be asked to calculate slope. They are shown in the examples below.

Example 1(Given two points):

Line A has points (3,-4) and (0,0). Line B has points (8,6) and (4,3). Determine the relationship of these lines.

    a. Parallel
    b. Perpendicular
    c. Intersecting
    d. Concurrent

To start, find the slope of each line using $\frac{y_1 - y_2}{x_1 - x_2}$. To stay organized, label your points

$$x_1\, y_1 \text{ and } x_2\, y_2$$
$$(3, -4) \quad (0,0)$$

Plug into the formula:

$$\frac{-4-0}{3-0} = \frac{-4}{3}\text{, which is the slope of line A.}$$

Repeat the process for line B:

$$x_1\, y_1 \text{ and } x_2\, y_2$$
$$(8,6) \quad (4,3)$$

Plug into the formula:

$$\frac{6-3}{8-4} = \frac{3}{4}\text{, which is the slope of line B.}$$

Now we can compare slopes. They are opposite reciprocals, so the lines are perpendicular.

Example 2

Use the formula

$$y = mx + b$$

What is the relationship between the two lines below?

$$5x + 2y = 10$$
$$-5x - 2y = 4$$

    a. Parallel
    b. Perpendicular
    c. Intersecting
    d. Concurrent

When given an equation of a line, you must put the equation in "y=" form to easily determine the slope. After rearranging, the equations look like:

$$y = -\frac{5}{2}x + 5$$

$$y = -\frac{5}{2}x - 2$$

The slopes are the value in front of the "x." In this case, the slopes are the same, therefore the lines are parallel.

GEOMETRY WORD PROBLEMS

Geometry word problems often have more than one step. It is important to organize the information you are given, determine the steps needed to find missing information, and answer what the question is asking.

Example: The perimeter of a rectangle is 52 ft. If the length is 10 less than 2 times the width, what is the width?

In this example, there are 3 clues: perimeter and length and type of shape. You can solve the problem with these 3 clues.

1. To find perimeter add all the lengths of the sides. When you add up the sides it equals 52.
2. The problem states that the length is 10 less than 2 times the width. $2w - 10$. Make sure when you see the words *less than,* you put the -10 in the right position in the equation.
3. The shape of the object is a rectangle. That means the widths are equal and the lengths are equal.

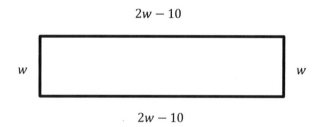

Perimeter requires you to add all the sides:

$2w - 10 + 2w - 10 + w + w = 52$

Write the equation like this

$$6w - 20 = 52$$

Add 16 from both sides

$$6w = 72$$

Solve for w

$$w = 12$$

Median: The me**d**ian is the mi**dd**le number (match your "d's").

1.   Arrange the data points in order from least to greatest.

2.   Find the middle number using one of the following methods-

   - Cross off one from the back and one from the front. Repeat this process until you are left with one or two numbers left.

   - Divide the number of points by 2.

** For odd numbers, you will be left with one number; that's the median.

**For even numbers, you will be left with two numbers. Add these two numbers and divide by 2 to find the median.

Mode: The m**o**de is the number that appears the m**o**st. It is possible to have no mode.

Mean: Mean is another word for average. $Average = \dfrac{sum}{number\ of\ terms}$

Range: To calculate the range of a set of data points, you find the difference of the largest number and the smallest number.

1.   Arrange data points in order from least to greatest.

2.   Subtract the largest number from the smallest number.

Strategies for Measures of Central Tendency

Some problems will be straightforward and ask you to calculate one of the measures of central tendency. Other problems will ask you to examine a set of data points and determine which measure of central tendency is the highest or give you a specific number and determine which measure of central tendency it is.

Be strategic!! Some problems will have anywhere from 15-30 data points. DO NOT spend the time writing out each number and calculating the mean. If you find that the mode and the median are the same values, eliminate both of them. There will never be two correct answers.

*For problems with all 4 measures of central tendency, you should NEVER be calculating the mean. Calculating the mean takes up time and there is a lot of room for error. The other 3 measures are easier to calculate and you can use process of elimination

Example 1:

A car company recorded the salaries for all of their employees, which are shown in the table below. They are advertising an opening and used $50,000 for the position. Which measure of central tendency did they use?

$40,000	$50,000	$60,000	$70,000	$100,000
4	4	5	1	1

    a. Mean

    b. Median

    c. Mode

    d. Range

For this problem, they are essentially asking, "Which measure of central tendency is $50,000?" DO NOT write out all of the numbers. You can eliminate mode right away because the salary that appears the most is $60,000. The range is also $60,000. To calculate the median, determine that the median will be the 8th number. In this case, the 8th number is $50,000, which matches the salary in the advertisement. The correct answer is B.

Example 2: There are 30 students in Mr. Richard's science class. On the last test, 3 of his students scored a 70%, 4 scored a 90%, and the rest of the students scored an 80%. Which measure of central tendency is the highest?

    a. Mean
    b. Median
    c. Mode
    d. Range

This is a problem where you need to be strategic. DO NOT write out all 30 numbers. Think of it in terms of frequency:

70%	80%	90%
3 students	23 students	4 students

Once you are looking at the data this way, it is easy to see that the median and the mode will both be 80%. Because they are the same, they both cannot be the correct answer, so eliminate them. The next easiest calculation is range. Here the range is 90-70= 20%. The mean will be greater than 20%, so eliminate range. You are only left with mean, which is the correct answer.

1. The length of a deck is 5 less than twice the width with a perimeter of 62 feet. What is the width of the deck rounded to the nearest tenth?

    A. 12.0
    B. 12.3
    C. 12.8
    D. 13.1

2. A car salesperson makes 30% commission from all sales during the month. His base pay is $240 per month plus what he makes on sales commission. Which of the following inequalities represents his pay at the end of the month so that he makes no less than $640?

    A. .3x + 240 < 640
    B. .3x + 240 > 640
    C. .3x + 240 ≤ 640
    D. .3x + 240 ≥ 640

3. Of the following, which number is greatest?

$$-12, -10, \frac{-21}{2}, -\sqrt{145}$$

    A. -12
    B. -10
    C. $\frac{-21}{2}$
    D. $-\sqrt{145}$

4. Put the following in order from least to greatest.

$$30\%, \frac{3}{4}, \frac{1}{3}, .8$$

    A. $\frac{1}{3}, \frac{3}{4}, .8, 30\%$

    B. $\frac{1}{3}, .8, \frac{3}{4}, 30\%$

    C. $30\%, \frac{1}{3}, .8, \frac{3}{4}$

    D. $30\%, \frac{1}{3}, \frac{3}{4}, .8$

5. A husband and wife share a cell phone plan where each is responsible for half the bill. The monthly base charge for service is $82. On top of the base charge, there are data charges, which each person is responsible for individually. At the end of the month, the total bill came to $120. If the husband is responsible for 60% of the data charges, how much does he owe for the month?

    A. $41.00
    B. $38.00
    C. $63.80
    D. $79.80

6. Mrs. Kramer, a first grade teacher, keeps a treasure box full of treats for students who answer the daily trivia question correctly. Today, Mindy answered correctly, so she gets to choose from the box, which was filled with 3 mints and 4 cookies. What is the probability she picks a mint?

    A. $\frac{1}{7}$
    B. $\frac{4}{7}$
    C. $\frac{3}{4}$
    D. $\frac{3}{7}$

7. On a trip from Naples to Tallahassee, a car travels a total of 500 miles at a rate of 55 mph. If the car gets 22 miles per gallon, how many gallons of gas will be consumed in 5 hours?

    A. 7.0 gallons
    B. 10.0 gallons
    C. 12.5 gallons
    D. 14.0 gallons

8. A triangle has interior angle measurements of 20°, 50°, and 110°. Classify the triangle.

    A. acute scalene
    B. isosceles
    C. obtuse scalene
    D. equilateral

9. If a textbook weighs $2\frac{1}{2}$ lbs. and notebooks weigh 4 oz., what is the total weight of 5 notebooks and 5 textbooks?

    A. $13\frac{1}{2}$ lbs
    B. $12\frac{1}{2}$ lbs
    C. $12\frac{3}{4}$ lbs
    D. $13\frac{3}{4}$ lbs

10. An Artist used a piece of wire that was 4 feet and 8 inches long and bent it into a square. What is the area of the square?

    A. $56\ in^2$

    B. $112\ in^2$

    C. $196\ in^2$

    D. $212\ in^2$

11. Mr. and Mrs. Morten have 5 children. Two of the children are 5 years old. The median age is 9 and the range of ages is 7. Which is a possible age of the second oldest Morten child?

    A. 2

    B. 4

    C. 9

    D. 14

12. Cosmo is taking a trip from his house to the airport. If he drives 60 mph, he will arrive 1 hour early. If he drives 30 mph, he will arrive 1 hour late. What is the distance from his house to the airport?

    A. 60 miles

    B. 120 miles

    C. 180 miles

    D. 240 miles

13. You and some friends decide to play a game of Frisbee. Person A starts by throwing the Frisbee 3 meters forward. Person B throws the Frisbee, and a gust of wind takes it 5 meters backward. Person C throws the Frisbee 2 meters forward. Finally, Person D throws the Frisbee up in the air, and it travels 1 meter forward. Where is the Frisbee in relation to the start?

    A. -1

    B. 0

    C. 1

    D. 3

14. Dimitri is shipping two boxes. The first box has dimensions of $2in$ x $8in$ x $6in$; the second box has dimensions $6in$ x $8in$ x $10in$. He puts both boxes into a third box, with dimensions of $12in$ x $12in$ x $12in$. How much empty space is left in the third box?

    A. $576\ in^3$

    B. $872\ in^3$

    C. $1,152\ in^3$

    D. $1,728\ in^3$

15. An office supply store it costs $24 for 16 pens. What proportion will find the cost for 21 pens?

    A. $\dfrac{24}{21} = \dfrac{16}{x}$

    B. $\dfrac{16}{24} = \dfrac{21}{x}$

    C. $\dfrac{16}{x} = \dfrac{21}{24}$

    D. $\dfrac{24}{16} = \dfrac{21}{x}$

16. Person 1 and Person 2 have each have annual salaries of $24,000. At the end of the year, they net a gross income of $56,000. Any monies collected after their salary is the result of a return on investments. What fraction of the year's total income is from investments?

A. $\frac{1}{7}$

B. $\frac{1}{8}$

C. $\frac{6}{7}$

D. $\frac{3}{8}$

17. Company A is hiring for many positions shown below in the salary chart. Given the information, what would be the best measure of central tendency that Company A would advertise to make the salary options look the best?

Salary/Year	$15,000	$20,000	$35,000	$100,000	$150,000
Positions available	1	4	7	1	1

A. Mean

B. Median

C. Mode

18. The range of teacher salaries is $40,000 to $60,000. During negotiations, the teacher's union worked out a deal for a flat raise of $1,000 for every teacher. Which of the following is true?

A. Mean and median salaries stay the same; standard deviation changes.

B. Mean and median salaries change; standard deviation stays the same.

C. Mean and median salaries change; standard deviation changes.

D. Mean and median salaries stay the same; standard deviation stays the same.

19. In a bag, there is 1 red marble, 1 yellow marble, 1 blue marble, and 1 green marble. After making a selection, the marble must stay out of the bag. How many possibilities are there when making two choices, the first being a red marble?

A. 2

B. 3

C. 4

D. 5

20. Which of the following choices falls between 0 and 2?

A. -4.037×10^3

B. 4.037×10^2

C. -4.037×10^{-2}

D. 4.037×10^{-3}

21. Classify the following:

$$3x + 2y = 6$$

$$-2x + 3y = 12$$

A. Parallel
B. Perpendicular
C. Parallel and intersecting
D. Concurrent

22. Solve:

$$5x - 7 \leq 2x - 10$$

A. $x \leq 1$
B. $x \leq -1$
C. $x \geq 1$
D. $x \geq -1$

23. Over the course of the school year in the JROTC class, Jenny logged the following totals of pull-ups: 2, 3, 22, 23, 23, 6, 8, 7, 9, 11, and 13. If she wanted to show the best-looking result, which measure of central tendency will she use?

A. Mean
B. Median
C. Mode
D. Range

24. Solve:

$$|6 - 8| + 3 \div 3 \times 4^2 - 2$$

A. 12
B. 16
C. 8
D. $\frac{1}{8}$

25. In the coordinate plane, which of the following is a function?

A. ellipse
B. horizontal line
C. circle
D. vertical line

26. The chart shows the results from an experiment where baking soda and ammonia were used as remedies for ant and tick bites. The time shown refers to when the pain subsided. According to the chart, which of the following statements is true?

	Ticks	Ants
Baking Soda	5 min	10 min
Ammonia	5 min	7 min

I.   Baking soda works better on ticks than ammonia.
II. Ammonia works better on ants than baking soda.
III. Ammonia works better than baking soda on both ants and ticks.
IV. If given the choice for the most effective remedy between the two, ammonia would be the best option.

   A. I only
   B. I and III
   C. II and IV
   D. IV only

27. The two charts above show two different companies' earnings over a period of time. Which of the following statements is true?

Company A	
Year	$ (Millions)
1	3
3	7
5	11
7	15

Company B	
Year	$ (Millions)
1	2
2	4
3	6
4	8

   A. Company A increased earnings $4 million per year.
   B. Company A's yearly earnings were greater than Company B's yearly earnings.
   C. Both companies had the same yearly earnings.
   D. Company B increased earnings $1 million per year.

28. Bayside High School has a student population of 1,400 with a teacher to student ratio of 1:35. How many more teachers must the principal hire in order to make the ratio 1:20?

   A. 40
   B. 70
   C. 30
   D. 20

29. During a homework check, you received the following problem. In which step, if any, did the student make a mistake?

$(x - 1)^2 - (x - 1)(x + 1)$

Step 1: $(x^2 - 2x + 1) - (x^2 - 1)$

Step 2: $x^2 - 2x + 1 - x^2 - 1$

Step 3: $-2x$

    A. Step 1
    B. Step 2
    C. Step 3
    D. No mistake was made.

30. Use the information to write an equation.

r	g
16	12
12	9
8	6
4	3

    A. $r = \frac{3}{4}g$
    B. $r = \frac{1}{3}g$
    C. $g = \frac{3}{4}r$
    D. $g = \frac{4}{3}r$

31. Which of the following statements below is true?

    A. $4^3 = 3^4$
    B. $5^0 \times 8^2 > 2^5$
    C. $7^4 + 7^3 = 7^7$
    D. $5^2 + 5^8 = 5^{10}$

32. Solve:

$$a^3 b^3 (ab)^{-2}$$

    A. ab

    B. $a^2 b^2$

    C. a

    D. b

33. A family wants to sod their 10 x 50 ft lawn. Sod is $3.00 per 10 $sqft$. How much will it cost the family to sod their entire lawn?

    A. $50.00

    B. $1,500.00

    C. $150.00

    D. $300.00

34. What is the name of a shape where:

- The bases (top and bottom) are parallel.
- One pair of interior angles are acute.
- One pair of interior angles are obtuse.
- The diagonals are congruent.

    A. Triangle

    B. Trapezoid

    C. Square

    D. Rectangle

35. If the total amount of money per month is $2,500, how much of the budget does the family spend on food and clothes?

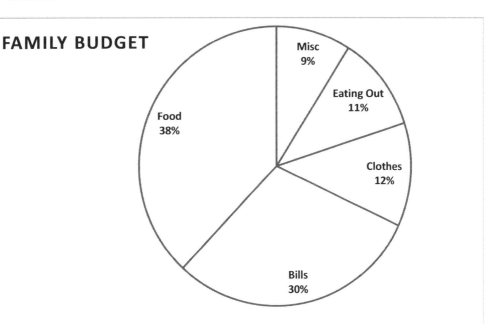

FAMILY BUDGET

Misc
9%

Eating Out
11%

Food
38%

Clothes
12%

Bills
30%

    A. $1,000
    B. $1,200
    C. $1,225
    D. $1,250

36. Out of 30 students, 1 scores 70%, 5 others score 90%, and the rest score 80%. Which of the following measures of central tendency has the highest value?

    A. Mean
    B. Median
    C. Mode
    D. Range

37. Nancy is putting an 8 x 10 picture in a frame. To make it fit, she needs to trim the sides. She takes 2.5 inches from the top and bottom. She takes .5 inches in from both sides. What is the area of the picture after she makes these changes?

    A. $56 \ in^2$
    B. $54 \ in^2$
    C. $42 \ in^2$
    D. $35 \ in^2$

38. Cindy is selling different necklaces at the flea market. She has two 15-inch necklaces, one 18-inch necklace, and two 20-inch necklaces. If she adds an additional 18-inch necklace and a 20-inch necklace, how does the mean change with all the necklaces?

    A. increase by 0.5
    B. decreased by 0.5
    C. increased by 0.4
    D. decreased by 0.4

39. Solve:

$$3 < 2x + 1 < 7$$

    A. $x = 1$
    B. $x = 2$
    C. $x = 3$
    D. $x = 4$

40. A baseball team has won 40% of the 40 games they have played so far. They have 70 more games to go. How many games do they need to win to win 70% of all the games in the season?

    A. 16
    B. 21
    C. 49
    D. 61

1.	**A**		24.	**B**
2.	**D**		25.	**B**
3.	**B**		26.	**C**
4.	**D**		27.	**C**
5.	**C**		28.	**C**
6.	**D**		29.	**B**
7.	**C**		30.	**C**
8.	**C**		31.	**B**
9.	**D**		32.	**A**
10.	**C**		33.	**C**
11.	**C**		34.	**B**
12.	**B**		35.	**D**
13.	**C**		36.	**A**
14.	**C**		37.	**D**
15.	**B**		38.	**C**
16.	**A**		39.	**B**
17.	**A**		40.	**D**
18.	**B**			
19.	**B**			
20.	**D**			
21.	**B**			
22.	**B**			
23.	**C**			

1.   **A**. This question is asking you to find the perimeter. Perimeter is the result of ADDING all the sides of the shape. In this case, we have a rectangular deck. The length is 5 less than twice the width, which is written $2w - 5$. And the width is just w.

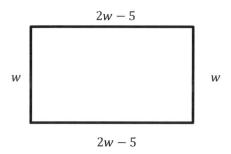

When you add up all the sides, you get:

$2w - 5 + 2w - 5 + w + w = 62$

$6w - 10 = 62$

Solve the equation by adding 10 to each side:

$6w - 10 = 62$

$6w = 72$

Divide each side by 6:

$w = 12$

2.   **D**. In this question, you are being asked to write an equation, not solve an equation. Pay attention to the very last line in the question, "...he makes NO LESS THAN $640?" Immediately eliminate any answer choice with a *less than* sign (<), so **A** and **C** are out. Then look at the *greater than* (>) signs in your answer choices. If he makes NO LESS than $640, that means he can make exactly $640 <u>and</u> he can make more than $640. So, the correct choice should be *greater than or equal to* (≥), and that makes **D** the correct choice.

3.   **B**. Pay attention to negative numbers here. -10 is greater than any of the other numbers: -12, $\frac{-21}{10} =$ $-10.5, -\sqrt{145} = -12.04$

4.   **D**. To put these numbers in order, convert them to decimals: 30% becomes .30, $\frac{3}{4}$ becomes .75, $\frac{1}{3}$ becomes .33 repeating, and .8 becomes .80 (same as .8). The order should be .30 (30%), .33 ($\frac{1}{3}$), .75 ($\frac{3}{4}$), .80 (.8).

5.   **C**. Each person is responsible for half the base charge of $82. Therefore, the husband pays $41 of the base charge. He also pays 60% of the data charges. To find the data charges, subtract the base charge from the whole bill $120 - $82 = $38.00. The husband pays 60% of $38.00, which is $22.80. Add $22.80 (his data) to the $41 for the base. The total is $63.80.

6. **D**. Use fractions for probability. Put the selected over the total. Because there are 3 mints out of 7 items in the treasure chest, the fraction is $\frac{3}{7}$.

7. **C**. There is extra information in this question that you do not need. The question is asking how many gallons will be burned in 5 hours, not the entire trip. Therefore, the 500 miles is irrelevant information. Use the formula $S = \frac{D}{T}$ (speed equals distance over time). The speed is 55, the time is 5 hours. Solve for D.

$$55 = \frac{D}{5}$$
$$D = 275$$

Divide 275 by 22 mpg, which gives you 12.5 gallons burned.

8. **C**. Pay attention to the obtuse angle mentioned - 110°. Choose the answer with the word *obtuse* in it.

9. **D**. Convert the weight of the textbooks to ounces. There are 16 oz in 1 lb. Therefore, $2\frac{1}{2}$ lbs is 40 oz. Multiply 5 times 40 (the textbooks) and 5 times 4 (the notebooks). That gives you 200 and 20, respectively. Together, the books and notebooks weigh 220 total oz. Divide 220 by 16 to convert the oz to lbs, which equals 13.75 or $13\frac{3}{4}$.

10. **C**. Convert the $4\,ft\,8\,in$ into inches, which is $56\,in$. A square has four equal sides, so divide 56 by 4, which gives you 14. Area is base times height, $14\,x\,14 = 196\,in^2$.

$$4\,ft\,8\,in = 56\,in$$

_____

$$56 \div 4 = 14$$

14

14   14

14

$$Area = base\ times\ height$$
$$(14\ X\ 14) = 196\ in^2$$

11. **C.**

5	5	9	X	?

We know the median is 9, so that number goes in the middle. The only place for the two 5-year-olds is before the 9. We do not yet know the age of the second oldest child or the age of the oldest child, but we do know the range is 7. The range is the biggest number minus the smallest. Therefore, if the range is 7 and the smallest number is 5, the last child is 12. The only number in the answer choice that will fit is 9.

12. **B**. If Cosmo goes 60 mph, he arrives an hour early; if he goes 30 mph, he arrives an hour late. That is a 2-hour difference in time. Use your answer choices to solve. 120 miles is the only answer that has a 2-hour difference.

$$\frac{120 \; miles}{60 \; mph} = 2 \; hours$$

$$\frac{120 \; miles}{30 \; mph} = 4 \; hours$$

13. **C**. Use a number line to answer this question. Start at zero and add or subtract based on the question. Zero up 3 is 3. From 3 back 5 is -2. From -2 up 2 is zero. From zero to 1 is 1.

14. **C**. Find the volume of all three boxes. The first box is 96. The second box is 480. Add them together to get 576. You put them in the big box, which is 1,728. So subtract the total of the two small boxes (576) from the big box (1,728). The answer is 1,152.

15. **B**. When solving proportions, make sure everything matches. For example, when using pens over dollars, the equation would be $\frac{16}{24} = \frac{21}{x}$. When using dollars over pens, the equation would be $\frac{24}{16} = \frac{x}{21}$. There is only one answer choice that keeps pens with pens and dollars with dollars, and that is **B.**

16. **A**. Just look at the main numbers without the zeros. Together, the couple makes 48 in income, but their gross income is 56. So subtract 48 from 56 and you get 8. So 8 comes from investments. Put 8 over the total and you get $\frac{8}{56}$. Then reduce the fraction to $\frac{1}{7}$.

17. **A**. For mean median and mode problems where there many numbers, try process of elimination. Also, do not factor in the zeros. You have 14 salaries – one 15, four 20s, seven 35s, one 100, and one 150. The number 35 is going to be the mode because it happens more frequently than any other number. If there are seven 35s out of the 14 numbers listed, then 35 is also the median. You can eliminate **B** and **C**. Therefore, A is your answer. Be strategic.

18. **B**. Let's factor this without the zeros. Let's say there are 3 teachers with salaries at 40, 50, and 60. The median of this set is 50 and the mean is 50. The standard deviation is 10 because there is a difference of 10 between each teacher: 40 to 50, and 50 to 60. If I give everyone a raise of 1, the set changes to 41 – 51 – 61. Notice the mean and median changed to 51, but the standard deviation is still 10 because 41 to 51 is 10, and 51 to 61 is 10.

19. **B**. If the first choice has to be red every time, there are only 3 possibilities: red – blue, red – yellow, red – green.

20. **D**. This is scientific notation. Move the decimal based on the exponent. If the exponent is negative, move the decimal to the left. If the decimal is positive, move the decimal to the right. D is the answer because 4.037×10^{-3} is $.004037$, which is between 0 and 2.

21. **B**. Use the equation $y = mx + b$ to find the slope of each line.

$$3x + 2y = 6 \qquad\qquad -2x + 3y = 12$$

$$y = -\frac{3}{2}x + 3 \qquad\qquad y = \frac{2}{3}x + 6$$

The slope of this line is $-\frac{3}{2}$. The slope of this line is $\frac{2}{3}$.

Because the slopes are the opposite reciprocal, they are perpendicular.

22. **B**. Get x on one side of the equation by subtracting 2x from both sides and adding 7 to both sides.

$5x - 7 \leq 2x - 10$ becomes

$3x \leq -3$

Solve for x.

$x \leq -1$

23. **C**. The mean is the most complicated to find, so try to find everything else first. In this set, the mode is the highest number – 23. We know the median is going to be less than 23, so median is out. The range will be less than 23 because the range is the biggest minus the smallest (23 – 2 = 21). The median is less than the mode as well. And the mean is going to be a number between 23 and 2. Therefore, mode is going to be your highest value in this set.

24. **B**. Use PEMDAS. Do the absolute value brackets first. The absolute value of $6 - 8$ is 2.

$$|6 - 8| + 3 \div 3 \times 4^2 - 2$$

$$2 + 3 \div 3 \times 4^2 - 2$$

Then do the exponent.

$$2 + 3 \div 3 \times 16 - 2$$

Then do the multiplication/division.

$$2 + 1 \times 16 - 2$$

$$2 + 16 - 2$$

Then do the addition and subtraction.

$$2 + 16 - 2 = 16$$

25. **B**. In a function, the x does NOT repeat. In an ellipse, the x repeats. In a circle, the x repeats. In a vertical line, the x repeats. However, in a horizontal line, the x does not repeat (the y does).

26. **C**. The only true statements are II and IV.

27. **C**. Look closely. Both companies show the same profits. The only difference is that Company A shows profits every two years, while Company B shows profits every year. However, they both yield $2 million every year. Company B yields $4 million every two years or $2 million every year.

28. **C**. This is a proportion. Currently, we have 1,400 students with a ratio of $\frac{1\ teacher}{35\ students}$. Set it up like this: $\frac{x}{1,400} = \frac{1}{35}$. Then cross multiply and solve.

$$35x = 1,400$$

$$x = 40$$

The desired ration in the school is $\frac{1\ Teacher}{20\ students}$. Solve the proportion this way. $\frac{x}{1,400} = \frac{1}{20}$. Cross multiply and solve.

$$20x = 1,400$$

$$x = 70$$

Because the principal already has 40 teachers and needs 70, he or she must hire 30 more teachers.

29. **B.** In the second step, the student did not distribute the negative sign all the way through the equation.

The student calculated this:

$$x^2 - 2x + 1 - x^2 - 1$$

The student should have gotten:

$$x^2 - 2x + 1 - x^2 + 1$$

30. **C.** In the table, g is smaller than r by $\frac{3}{4}$.

31. **B.** Remember, when adding exponents, you cannot combine. You can only combine exponents when multiplying. The only expression that is true in this case is B. Remember, anything to the exponent of 0 is 1.

32. **A.** Whenever solving anything to the -2, square it and put it under 1. For example: $3^{-2} = \frac{1}{9}$, $4^{-2} = \frac{1}{16}$, $5^{-2} = \frac{1}{25}$. Therefore: $(ab)^{-2} = \frac{1}{a^2 b^2}$

This becomes:

$$a^3 b^3 \times \frac{1}{a^2 b^2}.$$

$$\frac{a^3 b^3}{a^2 b^2} = ab$$

33. **C.** Find the area of the lawn, which is $50 \times 10 = 500$. Sod costs $3.00 per 10 $sqft$. So divide the 500 by 10, which gives you 50. Multiply the 50 by $3.00, which gives you $150.00.

34. **B.** If you draw this shape out, you will discover it is a trapezoid. The biggest give-away is the top and bottom are parallel, but one pair of interior angles are acute.

35. **D.** In this budget, 50% is spent on clothes and food. So multiply $2,500 by 50% or divide it by 2. That gives you $1,250.

36. **A.** This is another case where you do not have to write all these numbers down. The mode and the median are the same – 80%. So B and C are out. The range will be significantly smaller than the mean, so D is out. That leaves A.

37. **D**. If you subtract two, 2.5*in* from the top and two, 2.5*in* from the bottom, you took off 5*in* total. Also, two, .5*in* in from each side, is 1*in* from the sides. That means the 8 x 10 picture becomes a 5 x 7. Therefore, the area is 35.

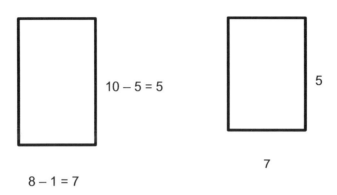

$$10 - 5 = 5$$

5

7

$$8 - 1 = 7$$

38. **C**. If you add lengths to the original, the mean goes up, not down. Therefore, you can eliminate **B** and **D**. The original mean is 15 + 15 + 18 + 20 + 20 = 88. Divide by 5 = 17.6. When you add the additional lengths (18 + 20) and divide by 7, you get 18.0. The difference is .4.

39. **B**. Use your answer choices and solve. The only one that works for x is 2.

$$3 < 2(2) + 1 < 7$$
$$3 < 5 < 7$$

40. **D**. If the baseball team won 40% of 40 games, they won 16 games (40% x 40 = 16). Their goals is to win 70% of the total games. If they have 70 more game to go, the total is 110 games because 40 + 70 = 110. Therefore, 70% of 110 is 77 games. They have already won 16, so they need to win 61 more games.

1. The width of a garden is 4 less than 3 times the length. If the perimeter of the garden is 32ft, what is the length of the garden?

    A. 2ft
    B. 3ft
    C. 5ft
    D. 9ft

2. Choose the greatest number:

    A. 6.4%
    B. $\sqrt{39}$
    C. $|-6.5|$
    D. $\frac{29}{5}$

3. Which symbol should be in the box?

$$-\frac{15}{8} \ [\ \ ] -\frac{34}{19}$$

    A. $<$
    B. $>$
    C. $=$
    D. $\approx$

4. Which symbol should be in the box?

$$1.34 \ x \ 10^{-2} [\ \ ] 134\%$$

    A. $<$
    B. $>$
    C. $=$
    D. $\approx$

5. Put the following numbers in order from least to greatest:

$$-.61, -\frac{2}{3}, -\frac{7}{11}, -.\overline{61}$$

A. $-.61, -\frac{2}{3}, -\frac{7}{11}, -.\overline{61}$

B. $-\frac{2}{3}, -\frac{7}{11}, -.\overline{61}, -.61$

C. $-.61, -.\overline{61}, -\frac{7}{11}, -\frac{2}{3}$

D. $-\frac{2}{3}, -\frac{7}{11}, -.61, -.\overline{61}$

6. In a bag of marbles, there are 2 blue marbles, 3 green marbles, and 7 yellow marbles. What is the probability of choosing a marble that is not yellow?

A. $\frac{5}{12}$

B. $\frac{7}{12}$

C. $\frac{1}{6}$

D. $\frac{2}{3}$

7. Ryan has an average of 88.6% in his math class after the first four tests. What does Ryan need to score on the 5th test to receive at least a 90% in the class?

A. 92%
B. 93.6%
C. 95.6%
D. 90%

8. Evaluate:

$$8^2 \div 4 + 4$$

A. 20
B. 8
C. 12
D. 48

9. Evaluate:

$$6^2 - 18 \div 3$$

A. 6
B. 9
C. 20
D. 30

10. Solve:

$$4n + 3 \geq 2n - 7$$

A. $n \geq 5$
B. $n \leq 5$
C. $n \leq -5$
D. $n \geq -5$

11. At Baymore High School, there is a ratio of 2:3 sophomore boys to sophomore girls. If there are 176 sophomore boys, how many sophomore girls are there?

    A. 264
    B. 352
    C. 117
    D. 100

12. Each year there is a Middle School Frisbee tournament. Player A throws the Frisbee and it ends up 2 feet behind the starting point. Player B picks it up and throws it 5 feet forward. Player C throws the Frisbee, which ends up 3 feet forward, but the wind then moves it a foot back. How far away from the starting position does the Frisbee end up?

    A. $5\,ft$
    B. $6\,ft$
    C. $10\,ft$
    D. $9\,ft$

13. There are 5 children in the Miller Family. The youngest two children are 4 years old. The median age is 6. If the range of ages is 7, what is a possible age for one of the older children?

    A. 12
    B. 5
    C. 10
    D. 13

14. After the storm, Julia's basement flooded with 18 inches of water. The water vacuum is able to clean 1.5 inches every 50 min. How long will it take Julia to clean all of the water?

    A. 8 hours
    B. 10 hours
    C. 12 hours
    D. 14 hours

15. A speed writing company advertised that their clients improve their typing speed to 1000 WPM after using their program. Below is the data from 8 clients. Which measure of central tendency would be the best to use if the CEOs wanted to make the company look the best use in their advertisement?

1000	700	1000	800
850	750	1050	950

    A. Median
    B. Mode
    C. Mean
    D. Range

16. Evaluate: $\frac{3}{4}a = 2(\frac{1}{2}a + 1)$

    A. -8

    B. $\frac{1}{4}$

    C. $-\frac{1}{4}$

    D. 4

17. Evaluate: $3(2 + a) = [6 - (2 - a)]$

    A. -1
    B. 1
    C. -2
    D. 2

18. Given the function $y - 2.45 = 14t + 18.3$, find the value of y when $t = .5$.

    A. 24
    B. 25.75
    C. 27.75
    D. 28.5

19. Mr. Parker had his 6th graders participate in a survey where they voted on their favorite non-team sport (Tennis, Golf, Swimming). He recorded the data in the bar graph shown below. Which is most deceiving about Mr. Parker's graph?

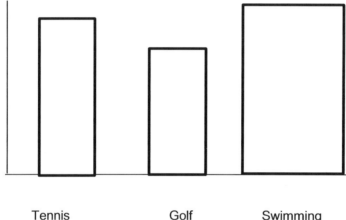

Tennis   Golf   Swimming

    A. There are no numbers on the vertical axis.
    B. There are categories on the horizontal axis instead of numbers.
    C. He did not put the results in ascending order.
    D. The width of the bars is not uniform.

20. Diana and Michele visited Illinois last week for 7 days. On the first day, the average temperature was 6 degrees. On the second day, the temperature was 10 degrees. The last two days of their trip, the temperature was –2 degrees. If on the other days, the average temperature was 3 degrees, what was the average temperature of their trip?

    A. 3°
    B. 4.5°
    C. 5°
    D. 5.25°

21. What is the median of the following data set?

    22, 18, 7, 16, 2, 17, 10, 7

    A. 8
    B. 9
    C. 13
    D. 14

22. Lee and Kate are selling their larger house in the country to move to a smaller house in the city. In the country, they paid for 1600 kilowatts of energy. In the city, they will pay for 800 kilowatts of energy. If the larger house cost them $.15 per kilowatt and the smaller house costs them $.10 per kilowatt, what is the percent decrease that they will pay for energy in the smaller house?

    A. 2%
    B. 33.3%
    C. 66.6%
    D. 92%

23. Miss Williams is collecting water from her lab groups after a science lesson. She collected the following amount of water from the groups: 4oz, 1c 3oz, 6 oz, 1c, 1oz, 2oz. How many cups of water did Miss Williams collect?

    A. 2 cups
    B. 3.5 cups
    C. 4 cups
    D. 4.5 cups

24. On a map, the shortest distance from Tampa to Miami is 4 inches. On this map, each ¾ inch is equivalent to 40 miles. If the actual distance from Tampa to Miami is 270 miles, what is the difference of the distance on the map from the actual distance?

    A. 6.75 miles
    B. 13.3 miles
    C. 56.7 miles
    D. 213.3 miles

25. Based on the following descriptions, which quadrilateral is described below?

    ▪ Opposite sides are parallel.
    ▪ All four sides are equal.
    ▪ One set of opposite sides are acute.

    A. Parallelogram
    B. Rhombus
    C. Square
    D. Trapezoid

26. Molly's bathroom floor is 6ft by 8ft. The tiles she picked out are 8in by 8 in. How many tiles will Molly have to buy?

    A. 81
    B. 108
    C. 216
    D. 432

27. When graphed on the coordinate plane, which represents a function?

    A. Circle
    B. Ellipse
    C. Vertical Line
    D. Horizontal Line

28. One interior angle of a triangle is $112°$. Classify this triangle.

    A. Acute
    B. Obtuse
    C. Right
    D. Equilateral

29. At which two points do $y = 2x^2$ and $y = 6x$ intersect?

    A. (0,0) and (3,18)
    B. (0,3) and (0,18)
    C. (0,18) and (0,0)
    D. (0,0) and (-3,-18)

30. Line A has points (0,-2) and (4,0) and line B has points (4,-2) and point (0,0). What type of relationship do the two lines shown below have?

    A. Intersecting
    B. Parallel
    C. Perpendicular
    D. Skew

31. Which is equivalent to $(4x + 1)^2$?

    A. $8x^2+1$
    B. $16x^2 + 1$
    C. $16x^2 + 8x + 1$
    D. $16x^2 + 4x + 1$

32. John makes a base pay of $280 a week and 30% commission on each of his sales. John needs to make at least $640 a week to pay for all of his bills. Which equation models this situation for John?

    A. $280 + .03c \leq 640$
    B. $280c + 30 \leq 640$
    C. $280 + .3c \leq 640$
    D. $280 + .3c \geq 640$

33. A car is 50 *lbs* less than a truck. Which of the following represents the weight of the car, c, in terms of the truck, *t?*

    A. $t = c - 50$
    B. $t = 50 - c$
    C. $c = 50 - t$
    D. $c = t - 50$

34. The following tables show the profits for two companies. Which statement is true regarding the data?

Company A

1	16
3	20
5	24
7	28

Company B

1	16
2	18
3	20
4	22

A. The rate of profit is greater for company A.
B. The rate of profit is greater for company B.
C. The rate of profit is equal for both companies
D. There is not enough information given to determine.

35. Angela recorded the number of hours she studied and the grades she received on each exam this year during finals, as shown in the table below. Which equation models the relationship between the number of hours she studied and the grade she received?

Number of Hours studied	Grade
1	60
2	70
3.5	85
4.5	95

A. $y = 50x + 10$
B. $y = 15x + 20$
C. $y = 1.5x + 55$
D. $y = 10x + 50$

NAVAED

36. Describe the trend of average temperature for Orlando from 1998 to 2006.

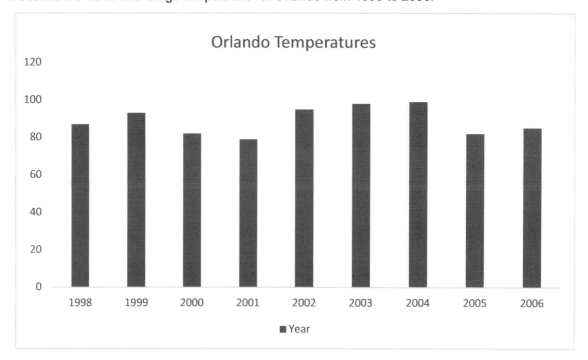

Orlando Temperatures

A. There is an increase in average temperatures from 1998 to 2006.
B. There is a decrease in average temperatures from 1998 to 2006.
C. The average temperature decreases and then increases.
D. There is no apparent trend in average temperatures from 1998 to 2006.

37. A carpenter bends a 5ft 8in wire into a square. What is the area of the square?

A. $56in^2$
B. $144in^2$
C. $196in^2$
D. $289in^2$

38. 1 middle school textbook weighs $1\frac{1}{2}lbs$ and 1 spiral notebook weighs 4oz. How much do 5 textbooks and 5 spiral notebooks weigh?

A. $7.5\ lbs$
B. $8\ lbs$
C. $8.75\ lbs$
D. $12.5\ lbs$

39. Evaluate:

$$-3 \leq 2x - 1 \leq 5$$

    A. $-1 \leq x \leq 3$

    B. $-\frac{3}{2} \leq x \leq 3$

    C. $\frac{1}{3} \leq x \leq \frac{9}{2}$

    D. 3

40. The following pie chart shows the number of TV sets per household for 2000 families. Given the data, how many households have at least 3 TV sets?

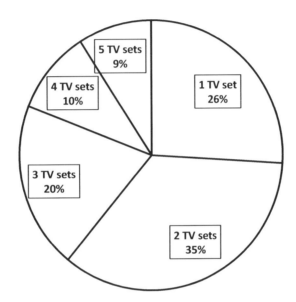

    A. 400
    B. 520
    C. 780
    D. 910

NAVAED

1.	C	24.	C
2.	C	25.	B
3.	A	26.	B
4.	A	27.	D
5.	B	28.	B
6.	A	29.	A
7.	C	30.	A
8.	A	31.	C
9.	D	32.	D
10.	D	33.	D
11.	A	34.	C
12.	A	35.	D
13.	C	36.	D
14.	B	37.	D
15.	B	38.	C
16.	A	39.	A
17.	A	40.	C
18.	C		
19.	D		
20.	A		
21.	C		
22.	C		
23.	C		

1. **C.** Set $w = 3l - 4$. Plug known values into the Perimeter formula, $P = 2l + 2w$:

$$32 = 2l + 2(3l - 4)$$
$$32 = 2l + 6l - 8$$
$$32 = 8l - 8$$
$$40 = 8l$$
$$L = 5$$

2. **C.** Put each number in decimal form so it is easier to compare. Choice C evaluates to 6.5, which is the greatest number.

3. **A.** Put each number in decimal form so it is easier to compare. -1.789 is greater than (further right on the number line) -1.875

4. **A.** Evaluate both sides. The exponent is negative on the left side, so move the decimal over 2 places to the left. To convert a percent into a decimal, divide by 100. 1.34 is greater than .0134

5. **B.** Write each in decimal form and then use a number line to put in order from -1 to 0.

6. **A.** Probability is $\frac{Desired}{total}$. There are 12 marbles total, so that goes in the denominator. Here, the desired outcome is not yellow. If 7 are yellow, then there are 5 marbles that are not yellow.

7. **C.** $Average = \frac{(88.6*4)+x}{5}$, where the average is 90.

$$90 * 5 = (88.6 * 4) + x$$
$$450 = 354.4 + x$$
$$X = 95.6$$

8. **A.** Use order of operations to first evaluate 64 then divide by 4 and add 4.

9. **D.** Use order of operations to first evaluate 36, then divide 18 by 3 and subtract.

10. **D.** Solve the inequality by combining like terms and solving for n. Subtract $2n$ from the right and left and you get $2n$. Subtract 3 from the left and right and you get -10. Then set it up. And divide by 2.

$$2n \geq -10$$
$$n \geq -5$$

11. **A.** Set up a proportion of boys: girls.

$$\frac{2}{3} = \frac{176}{g}$$

Cross multiply to get $176 * 3 = 2g$

Solve for g.

$$528 \div 2 = 264$$
$$g = 264$$

12. **A**. Count the feet the Frisbee moves or move across a number line.

Player A: -2 feet

Player B: +5 feet

Player C: +3 feet

Wind: -1

-2+5+3-1= 5 feet

13. **C**. Arrange the ages by what information is given. The youngest two children are 4. Because there are 5 children, the next oldest child is the median because that is the middle number. The range of the ages is 7, so the oldest child is 11 (4+7=11). Therefore, the second oldest child must be between ages 6 and 11.

14. **B**. This can be solved as a proportion using inches over time = inches over time $\frac{1.5}{50} = \frac{18}{x}$. Cross multiply and you get 1.5x = 900. Then divide both sides by 1.5, which equals 600 min. However, the answers are in hours. Therefore, you divide 600 by 60 (there are 60 min in an hour) and you get 10 hours.

15. **B**. The question is asking for 1000. The number 1000 happens in the set of numbers the most. Therefore, 1000 is the mode. [Median=900, Mean=887.5, Range=350]

16. **A**. Solve for a. Turn everything into a decimal. It becomes .75a = 2(.5a+1). Distribute the 2. You get .75a = 1a + 2. Then subtract 1a from both sides and you get -.25a = 1. Then divide by -.25 and you get a=-8.

17. **A**. Distribute on both sides. Be careful on the right side to distribute the negative to both the 2 and the -a. $6 + 3a = 6 - 2 + a$. Combine like terms and solve for a.

$$6 + 3a = 4 + a$$
$$2a = -2$$
$$a = -1$$

18. **C**. Plug .5 in for t and solve. $y - 2.45 = 14(.5) + 18.3$

$$y - 2.45 = 7 + 18.3$$
$$y - 2.45 = 25.3$$
$$y = 27.75$$

19. **D**. When creating graphs, the width of the bars must be uniform to accurately depict the data.

20. **A**. Find the average of the given temperatures: 6+10+-2+-2+3+3+3=21. 21/7=3

21. **C**. Arrange the numbers in order and find the middle number. There are an even number of data points, so add the middle two numbers together and divide by 2.

22. **C**. Find out how much they paid in the country by multiplying $1600(.15) = \$240$. Do the same for the city, $800(.10) = \$80$. $80\ is\ 33.33\%\ of\ 240$. To find the percent decrease, subtract $100\% - 33.3 = 66.7\%$

23. **C**. There are $8 \ oz \ in \ 1 \ cup$. Convert all cups into ounces and add:

$$4 \ oz \ + \ 11 \ oz \ + \ 6 \ oz \ + \ 8 \ oz \ + \ 1 \ oz \ + \ 2 \ oz \ = \ 32 \ oz$$

The answer choices are all in cups, so convert back to cups:

$$\frac{32}{8} = 4 \ cups$$

24. **C**. Find out how many miles are represented by 4 inches are equivalent to by setting up a proportion. $\frac{.75}{40} = \frac{4}{x}$. $X = 213.3333$ miles. Don't forget to subtract from 270 because the question is asking you the difference. Therefore, $270 - 213.3 = 56.7$.

25. **B**. In a rhombus all sides are equal, but the angles do not have to be equal. In a square, all sides are equal and all angles are equal. In a trapezoid, the top and bottom are not equal, so trapezoid is out. Therefore, rhombus is the answer.

26. **B**. Convert the dimensions of the floor from feet to inches first by multiplying each by $12in$ (there are 12 inches in a foot). Find the area of the bathroom floor $72 \times 96 = 6912$. Then divide by 64, the area of 1 tile ($8in \times 8in$). The answer is 108 tiles are needed.

27. **D**. A function must pass the "vertical line test." This means that when a vertical line is drawn at any point through the graph, the line will only pass through one point of the graph. Also, in a vertical line the x repeats. In a horizontal line, the y repeats. *In a function, the x cannot repeat.* Therefore, horizontal like is the answer.

28. **B**. 112 degrees is an obtuse angle (greater than 90 degrees), therefore the triangle is classified as obtuse.

29. **A**. Set both equations equal to each other. $2x^2 = 6x$. Then you realize it is a quadratic, which is

$$2x^2 - 6x = 0$$

Then factor the 2x out.

$$2x(x - 3) = 0$$

Set each section to zero:

$2x = 0$ solve for x.

$x = 0$

$(x - 3) - 0$ Solve for x.

$x = 3$

$x = 0 \ and \ x = 3$. *At this point, check your answer choices. Only one has x-values of both 0 and 3. If this were not the case, follow the remaining steps.

Plug both values into one of the equations to get the y-values.

6(0)=0 so one point is (0,0)   and 6(3)=18 so the other point is (3,18)

30. **A.** Slope is $\frac{y_1 - y_2}{x_1 - x_2}$. The words "parallel" and "perpendicular" are your clues to find the slope of each line. Therefore, the slope of line A is $\frac{-2-0}{0-4} = \frac{-2}{-4} = \frac{1}{2}$. The slope of line B is $\frac{-2-0}{4-0} = \frac{-1}{4} = -\frac{1}{2}$

The slope of line A is $\frac{1}{2}$. The slope of line B is $-\frac{1}{2}$. Recall that parallel slopes are the same and perpendicular slopes are opposite reciprocals of each other. These two slopes do not have either of these relationships, so they are intersecting.

31. **C.** $(4x + 1)(4x + 1)$ Expand. Now FOIL the two binomials.

$$16x^2 + 8x + 1$$

32. **D.** Write 30% as a decimal, .3. The variable is next to the percent commission. Since he needs AT LEAST $640, the quantity he makes needs to be larger than $640 or equal to $640.

33. **D.** Translate the sentence into an expression. Remember that with "less than," you must write it as the truck minus 50 or $t - 50$. Therefore, $c = t - 50$.

34. **C.** Find the rate of profit for both company A and company B by finding the common difference of each column. For company A, the rate of profit is $\frac{4}{2}$, *which simplifies to* $\frac{2}{1}$. For company B, the rate of profit is $\frac{2}{1}$. The rates of profit are equal.

35. **D.** Use your answer choices to plug in the x-values and y-values into each equation. The number of hours studied is the x value and grade is the y value. Plug in the x values into each of the equations given in the answer choices to see which equation is true for all values.

36. **D.** The data goes up and down without forming a pattern. Therefore, there is no trend in the data. In addition, all the other statements are false.

37. **D.** Convert $5ft\ 8in$ into inches, which is $68\ in$. A square has four equal sides, so divide $68ft$ by 4 to get the measure of side length, which is $17in$. Multiply $17in\ x\ 147in$ to get the area $289in^2$.

38. **C.** $1\ lb = 16\ oz$. Multiply 1.5 $lbs \times 5$ to get the weight of the textbooks. $4oz$ is equivalent to $.25lb$, so multiply $5 \times .25$. Add these two totals together to get the total weight.

39. **A.** Solve for x by using algebra.

$$-3 \leq 2x - 1 \leq 5$$

Add 1 to all sides of the inequality sings to isolate the variable.

$$-2 \leq 2x \leq 6$$

Divide all sides by 2 to solve for x.

$$-1 \leq x \leq 3$$

The only answer choice with that solution is A.

40. **C.** Add up the percents that have at least 3 TV sets, $20\% + 10\% + 9\% = 39\%$. Now find 39% of 2000 ($.39\ x\ 2000$) $= 780$.

1. Classify the triangle below

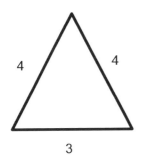

4   4

3

   A. equilateral

   B. scalene

   C. isosceles

   D. obtuse

2. Solve: $7 - (-1)^3 + 2 - 2$

   A. 9

   B. 8

   C. 6

   D. 4

3. Which of the following group of test scores has a range and median that are equal?

   A. 20, 30, 50, 70, 80

   B. 20, 40, 60, 70, 80

   C. 20, 40, 60, 80, 90

   D. 30, 50, 50, 80, 90

4. Solve: $(3 + 3 - 4) \div 2 - 3$

   A. 1

   B. 2

   C. −1

   D. −2

5. Solve for x by rounding to the nearest tenth: $5 - x = \sqrt{5}$

    A. 2.8

    B. −2.8

    C. −2.5

    D. 5.0

6. Which of the following is a function?

    A. (3, 4), (-2, 1), (-3, 5), (4, -2)

    B. (2, 2), (3, 2), (2, -1), (4, 2)

    C. (3, -4), (4, 3), (3, -8), (2, -1)

    D. (4, 1), (4, 5), (4, -2), (4, 0)

7. Solve: $5 + 3\,(2a) = 6[2a - (2 - a)]$

    A. $\dfrac{12}{7}$

    B. $\dfrac{17}{12}$

    C. $\dfrac{6}{5}$

    D. $\dfrac{5}{7}$

8. Estimate the lake's perimeter.

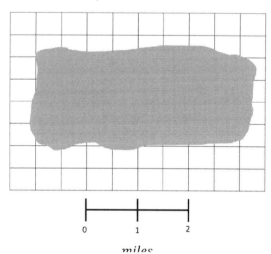

    0   1   2

    miles

    A. 8 miles

    B. 10 miles

    C. 12 miles

    D. 22 miles

9. Select the correct sign to go in the box below.

$$-\frac{1}{3} \; [\;] \; -\frac{2}{9}$$

A. <

B. >

C. ≤

D. ≥

10. Which of the following statements is true for the data set below?

20, 30, 50, 90, 90

A. The median is more than the mean.

B. The mean is more than the median.

C. The mode is less that the range.

D. The mode is less than the mean.

11. A husband and wife are going over their finances for the year in terms of their total income, including investments. At the end of the year, they have a total of $84,000 of combined total income. If they both make the same amount per year—$36,000—what percentage of their income came from investments.

A. 12%

B. 14%

C. 42%

D. 50%

12. Suzie is tiling her kitchen floor. The floor has an area of $10ft \times 7ft$. The tiles are $8in \times 8in$. How many tiles will she need for her entire kitchen floor?

A. 11

B. 12

C. 158

D. 1057

13. The chart below represents 6 different employees at a law firm. What measure of central tendency is the most accurate representation of salaries according to the chart below?

A. median

B. mean

C. mode

D. range

Person	Salary
1	34,000
2	36,000
3	37,000
4	40,000
5	50,000
6	1,500,000

NAVAED

14. The following line graph shows production of sprockets during a normal work week. Which of the following is true based on the data in the line graph below?

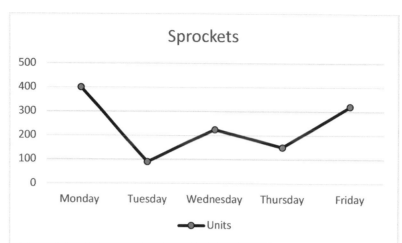

A. More sprockets were produced on Thursday than on Monday.

B. Fewer sprockets were produced on Monday than Wednesday.

C. There were never fewer than 150 sprockets produced on any given day.

D. Production of sprockets was higher on Friday than on Tuesday.

15. Bob take a legal-size piece of paper that measures $8.5in \times 14in$ and cuts $3in$ squares out of each corner. He then takes what is left and folds each tab upward, making a rectangular box with no lid. What is the volume of the box?

A. $181.5\ in^3$

B. $101.5\ in^3$

C. $88\ in^3$

D. $60\ in^3$

16. Which of the following is true based on the information given below?

Line A	
x	y
-10	3
-1	11

Line B	
x	y
8	4
2	9

A. Line A and B both increase; line A increases faster than line B.

B. Line A and B both decrease; line B decreases faster than line A.

C. Line A increases faster than line B decreases.

D. Line B decreases faster than line A increases.

17. Which of the following is true about the data set below?

1, 11, 9, 11, 5, 17, 5, 11, 2, 11

A. The mode is greater than the median.

B. The median is greater than the mode.

C. The mode is greater than the range.

D. The median is greater than the range.

18. The amount of recycled goods collected over the last twenty years at J & K Recycle Company is represented in the bar graph below. What is the problem with the way the information is presented in the graph below.

A. The title of the graph does not represent the data correctly.

B. The x axis does is not in chronological order.

C. The y axis does not increase in even increments.

D. The units of measure are not the same.

19. The end of a 15-foot ladder rests on the top of a 12-foot wall. What is the distance between the bottom of the wall and the bottom of the ladder?

A. $9\ feet$

B. $19\ feet$

C. $13.5\ feet$

D. $7\ feet$

20. Mr. Rodriguez just administered a chapter test to his 25 students. Five students received a 40%. One student received an 80%. The rest of the students received a 70%. Using this information, what measure of central tendency would showcase the highest value for this data set.

A. median

B. range

C. mean

D. minimum

21. A non-partisan organization is conducting a political poll to see which candidate voters are more likely to choose. What would be the most effective way to conduct the poll?

   A. Go to a local mall and randomly poll people walking by.

   B. Survey every 5th person who walks by at a park.

   C. Look at previous data and make predictions.

   D. Survey every 5th registered voter in the area.

22. The graph below represents the amounts of soybean and corn a farmer can buy. What does the y-intercept represent in the line graph below?

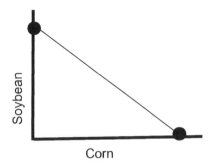

Corn

   A. The maximum amount of soybean the farmer can buy without buying any corn.

   B. The maximum amount of corn the farmer can buy without buying any soybean.

   C. The minimum amount of soybean the farmer can buy without buying any corn.

   D. The minimum amount of corn the farmer can buy without buying any soybean

23. A scientist is testing different brands of face creams—brands L, M, X, O. She is conducting the experiment in pairs. For example, how does brand L compare to brand M. How many tests will it take to test all face creams against one another?

   A. 6

   B. 8

   C. 10

   D. 12

24. Which of the following songs is the longest?

   A. Song A is $2.175 \ min$

   B. Song B is $3\frac{1}{8} \ min$

   C. Song C is $3\frac{1}{7} \ min$

   D. Song D is $3.5 \ min$

25. For work last month, Gwen made 4 trips that were 175 miles each and 3 trips that were 500 miles each. She spent $700 total on gas for the month. If she gets $.50 per mile from her boss, how much money does she have left over after she has paid for gas?

   A. $200

   B. $300

   C. $400

   D. $500

26. Which of the following is a function?

A.

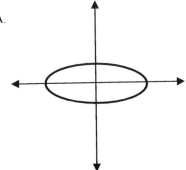

B.

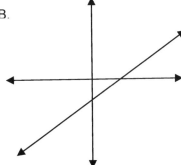

C.

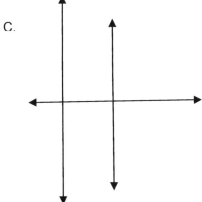

D.

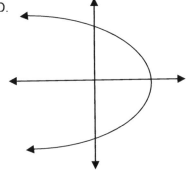

27. Which of the following is NOT a function?

A.

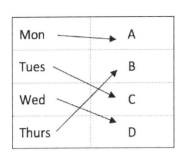

B.

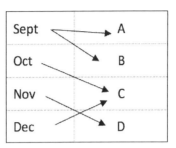

C.

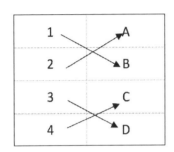

D.

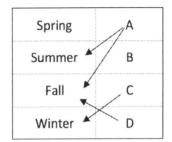

28. Which of the following equation represents 5 less than twice a number?

   A. $2n - 5$

   B. $5n - 2$

   C. $5 - 2n$

   D. $2 - 5n$

29. What is the angle measure for x?

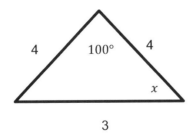

   A. 20°

   B. 30°

   C. 40°

   D. 50°

30. Evaluate the student's process below for the math problem below. At what step did the student make the mistake?

$$2(x + 4) - 3(x + 1)$$

step 1: $2x + 8 - 3(x + 1)$

step 2: $2x + 8 - 3x + 3$

step 3: $-x + 11$

A. step 1

B. step 2

C. step 3

D. no mistake

31. Susie is building a ramp. The instructions state that for every 4in high the ramp must be 6in long. Susie wants to build a ramp that is 1 ½ ft high. How long must the ramp be?

A. $24in$

B. $27in$

C. $36in$

D. $48in$

32. Line A has coordinates (5, -1) and (2, 4). Line B has coordinates (-3, 2) and (1, 1). Find the slope of Line A and B and determine the relationship of line A and B.

A. Line A has a slope of $-\frac{5}{3}$ and Line B has a slope of $-\frac{1}{4}$. Therefore, the lines are intersecting.

B. Line A has a slope of $-\frac{3}{5}$ and Line B has a slope of $-\frac{4}{1}$. Therefore, the lines are intersecting.

C. Line A has a slope of $-\frac{5}{3}$ and Line B has a slope of $\frac{3}{5}$. Therefore, the lines are perpendicular.

D. Line A has a slope of $-\frac{5}{3}$ and Line B has a slope of $-\frac{5}{3}$. Therefore, the lines are parallel.

33. The regular price of a mountain bike is $1400, and the regular price of its accompanying outdoor backpack is $200. The sporting goods store is offering a promotion; when the bike and the backpack are purchased together, the customer will receive 40% off the backpack. Calculate the total cost of the bike and the backpack at the promotional price.

A. $760

B. $1480

C. $1520

D. $1600

34. A homeowner wants to put a fence around her yard. It will take 300 meters of fencing. If one side of her rectangular yard is 70 meters, find the area of the yard.

   A. $160\ m^2$

   B. $300\ m^2$

   C. $1400\ m^2$

   D. $5600\ m^2$

35. Which of the following could be a solution to the inequality below?

   $$-5 \leq 2x - 1 < 5$$

   A. 2

   B. 5

   C. 7

   D. -5

36. James has a treasure chest full of trinkets. He has 17 toy cars, 5 tiny swords, 6 blue Legos, and 20 marbles. He randomly reaches in and pulls out a trinket. What is the probability he will pull out a blue Lego?

   A. $\frac{1}{8}$

   B. $\frac{2}{3}$

   C. $\frac{1}{2}$

   D. $\frac{17}{48}$

37. Solve for x.

   $$\frac{5x - 3}{5} = 2x + 1$$

   A. $-1\frac{3}{5}$

   B. $1\frac{3}{4}$

   C. $-\frac{4}{5}$

   D. $\frac{4}{5}$

38. Classify the two lines below.

Line A	Line B
$5x + 3y = 15$	$-3x + 5y = 12$

   A. parallel

   B. perpendicular

   C. intersecting

   D. concurrent

39. The ratio of boys to girls at the state college is 3:5. If there are 575 girls at the college, how many boys are there?

   A. 300

   B. 325

   C. 345

   D. 425

40. Jim is filling up his $8ft \times 10ft$ pool for the summer. He will fill it all the way up, leaving only 6 *inches* from the top of the pool. If the pool is $6ft$ deep, how many cubic ft of water will he use to fill his pool?

   A. $540 \ ft^3$

   B. $480 \ ft^3$

   C. $440 \ ft^3$

   D. $400 \ ft^3$

1. C	8. C	15. D	22. A	29. C	36. A
2. B	9. A	16. C	23. A	30. B	37. A
3. B	10. B	17. A	24. D	31. B	38. B
4. D	11. B	18. D	25. C	32. A	39. C
5. A	12. C	19. A	26. B	33. C	40. C
6. A	13. A	20. A	27. B	34. D	
7. B	14. D	21. D	28. A	35. A	

1. **C**. In an equilateral triangle, all sides are the same (the name is equal). In this figure only two sides are equal. In a scalene triangle, no sides are equal. There is not enough information to determine if this triangle is obtuse (containing an angle that is greater than 90 degrees). In an isosceles triangle, two sides are equal, and that is what's pictured here.

2. **B**. Use PEMDAS here.

$$Take\ -1\ to\ the\ third\ power, and\ you\ get\ -1.$$

$$(-1)(-1)(-1) = -1$$

$$Now\ work\ the\ problem\ left\ to\ right.$$

$$7--1+2-2$$

$$which\ is:$$

$$7+1+2-2=8$$

3. **B**. The range is the largest number minus the smallest in the set. The median is the middle number. Calculate the range first and see if it matches the middle number. In answer choice B, 60 is the median (middle number) and the range is 60 too ($80-20=60$).

4. **D**. Use PEMDAS here.

$$First\ do\ the\ parentheses.$$

$$(3+3-4) \div 2 - 3$$

$$2 \div 2 - 3$$

$$Next\ do\ the\ division$$

$$2 \div 2 - 3$$

$$1 - 3 = -2$$

5. **A**. Use your calculator here. Input $\sqrt{5}$ into your calculator (every calculator is different, so be sure you know how to do this). Round the answer you get to the nearest tenth. You get 2.2. Now solve the problem using algebra.

$$5 - x = 2.2$$

$$-x = -2.8$$

$$Change\ the\ negative\ variable\ by\ dividing\ both\ sides\ by\ -1.$$

$$x = 2.8$$

6. **A**. Remember, in a function the x-coordinate does **NOT** repeat. The x coordinate is the first number in the parentheses. Answer choice A is the only group of coordinates where the first number is not repeated in any of the other sets of numbers. Therefore, A is a function.

7. **B**. Use PEMDAS here. Remember, when you are faced with parentheses inside of parentheses, work from inside out.

$$5 + 3\,(2a) = 6[2a - (2 - a)]$$

$$5 + (6a) = 6(2a - 2 + a)$$

$$5 + 6a = 12a - 12 + 6a$$

Now combine like terms.

$$5 + 6a = 18a - 12$$

Now use algebra to solve.

$$5 + 6a = 18a - 12$$

$$17 = 12a$$

Solve for a by dividing both sides by 12.

$$\frac{17}{12} = a$$

8. **C**. Look at the scale below the picture. You will notice that 2 blocks equal 1 mile, so count each square and divide by 2. As you count around there are 8 on the top, 4 on the left, 8 on the bottom, and 4 on the right. $8 + 4 + 8 + 4 = 24$, divide by 2 and get 12 *miles*.

9. **A**. Quickly input the fractions into your calculator to get the decimal version. -0.333 is smaller than -0.222; therefore, it is less than (<).

10. **B**. The data set only consists of five numbers, therefore it is not as difficult to figure out the all the measures of central tendency. Range is $90 - 20 = 70$, Mode is 90, Median is 50, and Mean is $\frac{20+30+50+90+90=280}{5} = 56$. B must be the answer because 56 is larger than 50.

11. **B**. It is important to understand that there are two factors that go into combined income, salary and investments. The problem states that the couple make $36,000 each. When this is added together their combined income off of salary is $72,000. Since the end of year income was $84,000, you must subtract $72,000 in order to get the total money made off of investments. 84,000-72,000=12,000. To find the percentage of income that came from investments, you must take the amount of investments over total income. Use your calculator to solve $\frac{12,000}{84,000} = 0.14$. Since it is a decimal and they are asking for percent, move the decimal 2 places to the right.

12. **C**. First notice that there are two different units of measure in the problem. In order to avoid decimals, convert larger units into smaller ones, in this case feet to inches. There are 12 *inches* in a foot, therefore $10ft\ x\ 7ft$ becomes 120 inches and 84 inches. Next, find the area of the floor and then divide it by the area of the tile.

$$120\ x\ 84 = 10080;$$

$$8\ x\ 8 = 64;$$

$$\frac{10080}{64} = 157.5$$

Notice that the answer is not a whole number. There is no such thing as a fraction of a tile, therefor always round up to the next whole number for an answer of 158 tiles.

13. **A**. At first glance all of the salaries look very similar. Pay attention to the 1,500,000, it is going to skew the data in terms of the mean. Think about it, if you took the lowest and highest salaries and averaged the out in your head it would be way more than 50,000. Right away, mean is eliminated because it is too high. Next go through the answer choices and choose the best one that fits.

$$\text{Median is } \frac{37,000+40,000}{2} = 38,500$$

There is no mode.

Range $1,500,000 - 34,000 = 1,466,000$.

$38,500 best represents what a salary would be at this law firm.

14. **D**. Carefully read through the answer choices and see if they are true according to the graph. Choice A should say less instead of more, Choice B should say more instead of fewer, Choice C should say 100 instead of 150, which means D is correct. Friday's total was higher than Tuesday.

15. **D**. In order to fully understand this problem, draw a picture. Understand that 3 inches is going to be removed at each corner which is going to be a total of 6 inches off of the dimensions of all sides. If the paper is $8.5 \, x \, 14$, after the cuts are made the new dimensions become $2.5 \, x \, 8$.

$$8.5 - 6 = 2.5 \text{ and } 14 - 6 = 8.$$

The paper is then folded upward to create a rectangular box with no lid, think of a shoebox without the top. As the paper is folded, it now has a height of $3 \, inches$.

To find volume use $l \, x \, w \, x \, h$

$$2.5 \, x \, 8 \, x \, 3 = 60.$$

16. **C**. First find the slope of each line using the formula $\frac{y1-y2}{x1-x2}$. The closer the number is to one, the faster the slope.

For line A take $\frac{3-11}{-10-1} = \frac{-8}{-9} = \frac{8}{9}$

For line B take $\frac{4-9}{8-2} = \frac{-5}{6} = -\frac{5}{6}$

Whichever line is closest to 1 is increasing or decreasing faster. To see which one is closest to 1 use your calculator to divide the fractions. $8 \div 9 = 0.88, -5 \div 6 = .-0.83$. In this case, 0.88 is closer to one than -0.83. Line A has a slope of $\frac{8}{9}$, which is a positive slope, so A is increasing. Line B has a slope of $-\frac{5}{6}$, which is a negative slope, so it is decreasing. Therefore, A is increasing faster than B decreases because A's slope is closer to 1.

17. **A**. First put the numbers in order: 1, 2, 5, 5, 9, 11, 11, 11, 11, 17. In this set, the mode is 11, the median is 10 (because the set of numbers is even, you take the two middle numbers, add them, and divide by 2), the range is 16, and the mean is 8.3. Based on this, A is the true statement in the answer choices.

18. **D**. Look at the bars and you will see that all but one are measured in grams. One is measured in ounces. All units of measure should be the same when comparing in a graph.

19. **A**. Turn this word problem into a triangle and use the Pythagorean Theorem to solve.

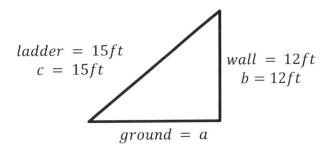

$ladder = 15ft$
$c = 15ft$

$wall = 12ft$
$b = 12ft$

$ground = a$

Pythagorean Theorem is $a^2 + b^2 = c^2$

c is always your hypotenuse.

$$a^2 + 12^2 = 15^2$$
$$a^2 + 144 = 225$$

$$a^2 = 81$$

$$a = 9$$

20. **A**. When you are faced with a central tendency problem where there are more than 10-15 numbers look at the mode and the median. Many times, they will be the same. And you can see in this problem they are the same.

40% - 5 students

70% - 19 students

80% - 1 student

You can see that 70% is the median. Now calculate the range (the biggest number minus the smallest number, which is $80\% - 40\% = 40\%$. The mean (average) can be calculated by adding all the numbers and dividing by 25. $5(40) + 19(70) + 1(80) = 1610$ and divide by 25 (total number of people). That equals 64.4%, which is smaller than the median (70%). Therefore, the median is the biggest choice out of the 4 answer choices. Quick tip: minimum is not something you would use for central tendency.

21. **D**. This question deals with statistical sample populations. In order for the poll to be effective, the persons polled must have be consistent. In example A, polling random people at a mall may get you all teenagers or all old people. For answer B, if there are all children playing at a park it is not a good sample population. Finally, previous data is not useful for a poll. Surveying every fifth person provides consistency and a good sample population.

22. **A**. The y-intercept is the key to this question. The y-intercept is the vertical axis which is labeled soybean. Where the line of the graph touches the y-axis determines the amount of soybean that can be purchased. According to the graph, this is the maximum for soybean and minimum, or zero amount, of corn.

23. **A**. To solve this problem, you can simulate the trials. Start with a letter and pair it with each one without repeating. Continue until there are no more letters.

LM	LX	LO
MX	MO	XO

24. **D**. Use your calculator to determine the decimal form of the two fractions. Once this is done you will see that 3.5 is the highest number.

25. **C**. In this problem, Gwen's income is based on every mile driven. To calculate this, we must figure out her mileage for the month.

$$\text{Mileage is } 4 \, x \, 175 = 700 \text{ and } 3 \, x \, 500 = 1500;$$

$$\text{Then add them together to get the total mileage - } 700 + 1500 = 2200.$$

$$\text{Since she is paid } \$0.50 \, per \, mile, \text{take } 2200 \, x \, 0.50 = 1100.$$

$$\text{Taking away her gas expenses will leave you with } \$1100 - \$700 = \$400.$$

26. **B**. For this type of problem remember, the x does NOT repeat in a function. When you are presented with a function problem with image son a graph like this, do the vertical line test. That means draw a vertical line (in red below) through the graph and see if the line goes through two points in the shape on the graph. You can see below, B is the only graph where the vertical line does NOT hit two points.

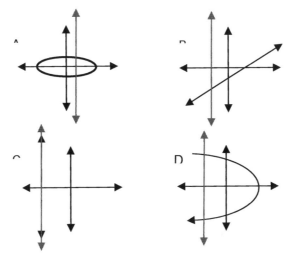

27. **B**. These charts represent functions. The left column is the x-coordinate and the right column is the y-coordinate. Remember, **functions never repeat the x-coordinate**. In order for that to work is to illustrate only one arrow to or from each item on the left column. Answer B has two arrows for September which means it repeats itself. Therefore, B is NOT a function.

28. **A**. Be careful when reading this question and writing the equation literally. 5 less than means to take five away from a value not the other way around. Therefore, $5 \, less \, than \, is \, -5$. So $2n - 5$ is the correct answer choice.

29. **C**. First, it is important to classify the triangle in order to decide what strategy to use. Since both legs have values of 4, it means that this is an isosceles triangle. By definition, isosceles triangles have two sides that are the same and two base angles that are the same. To calculate angle measure you need to know all angle measures add up to $180°$. Since one angle is already $100°$ degrees, we must subtract that from $180°$ to get $80°$. Since we know base angles are the same we must divide $80°$ by 2. $(80 \div 2 = 40)$ to get the measure of only one, x. The two bottom angels are $40°$ each. Therefore, $x = 40°$.

30. **B**. For this problem make sure you watch the distribution of the values to make sure it is correct. A giveaway is the negative sign before the 3. The negative must be distributed correctly, which in this case is not what happened in step 2. Most of the time in these student error problems, the mistake happens in the PEMDAS or the distribution. If you see a negative sign before a parenthesis, most of the time the issue is with distribution.

31. **B**. Use proportions to solve this problem. Since it states height of ramp then length, that is how your proportion will be setup. Don't forget that the units are not the same and must be converted. Convert feet to inches for the height of the new ramp (1.5 x 12=18). Set all heights on the top and length on the bottom

$$\frac{height}{length} \quad \frac{4}{6} = \frac{18}{x}$$

Cross-multiply $108 = 4x$

Solve for x by dividing

$$x = \frac{108}{4}$$

$$x = 27$$

32. **A**. In order to solve this problem, you have to find the slope of both sets of coordinates given. To do this use the formula $\frac{y1-y2}{x1-x2}$. Line A $\frac{(-1-4)}{(5-2)} = -\frac{5}{3}$ Line B $\frac{(2-1)}{(-3-1)} = -\frac{1}{4}$

Since the slopes are not the same, the lines are not parallel. They are also not opposite reciprocals which means they are not perpendicular. The two lines will eventually intersect.

33. **C**. Since you are getting the promotional price for the backpack, you have to figure out the discount. 40% off of the backpack is $0.4 \times 200 = 80$. Subtract 80 from the cost to get the discounted price of $200 - 80 = 120$. Add 120 to the cost of the bike ($1400) to get the total price.

$$\$120 + \$1400 = \$1520.$$

34. **D**. To solve this problem you must know the property of a rectangle that states opposite sides are congruent (same). If one side is $70\ meters$ that means the opposite side is $70\ meters$ for a total of $140\ meters$. Since there is $300\ meters$ total, we must subtract 140 in order to get the remaining side lengths,

$$300 - 140 = 160$$

160 is the total for both sides. Therefore, we have to divide by 2.

$$\frac{160}{2} = 80.$$

Now that we know the dimensions of the yard, we can find area.

$$Area = b \times h$$

$$70 \times 80 = 5600$$

35. **A**. The quickest way to solve this problem is to use guess and check. Substitute each answer choice for x and determine which value makes the inequality true.

36. **A.** To determine probability, you need to set up a ratio (fraction) with the amount of the chosen item as the numerator (top) and the entire sample size as the denominator (bottom). Since there are 6 Legos and 48 total pieces the ratio is $\frac{6}{48}$. Always check and see if it can be reduced, in this case it can, $\frac{1}{8}$.

37. **A.** The first step to solving this problem is to multiply the entire equation by 5 to get rid of the 5 in the denominator.

$$\frac{(5x-3)}{5} = (2x+1)$$

$$5 \bullet \frac{(5x-3)}{5} = (2x+1) \bullet 5$$

$$5x - 3 = 10x + 5$$

Use algebra to get the variable on one side of the equal sign and the integers on the other.

$$-8 = 5x$$

$$x = -\frac{8}{5} \ or \ -1\frac{3}{5}$$

38. **B.** In order to classify the lines, you must determine the slopes of each line. Lines that have the same slope are parallel, lines that have slopes that are opposite reciprocals are perpendicular. Make sure to use the slope-intercept form $y = mx + b$ to convert each equation.

Line A

$$5x + 3y = 15$$

$$3y = -5x + 15$$

$$y = -\frac{5}{3}x + \frac{15}{3}$$

Line B

$$-3x + 5y = 12$$

$$5y = 3x + 12$$

$$y = \frac{3}{5} + \frac{12}{5}$$

The slope of line A is $-\frac{5}{3}$.

The slope of line B is $\frac{3}{5}$.

Comparing the two slopes you will notice that they are opposite reciprocals and therefore perpendicular lines.

39. **C.** Use a proportion to solve this problem. Since it states boys to girls, then the ratio is going to be $\frac{boys}{girls}$.

$$\frac{3}{5} = \frac{x}{575}$$

$$5x = 1725$$

$$x = 345$$

40. **C.** This is a volume problem which means to multiply L x W x H. Make sure you understand that the dimensions are in feet and the 6 inches from the top is in a different unit. 6 inches is ½ a foot, so the height of the pool is 5.5. Multiply $8 \ x \ 10 \ x \ 5.5 = 440$.

GKT ESSAY

- Determine the purpose of writing to task and audience.

- Provide a section that effectively introduces the topic.

- Formulate a relevant thesis or claim.

- Organize ideas and details effectively.

- Provide adequate, relevant support by citing ample textual evidence; response may also include anecdotal experience for added support.

- Use of a variety of transitional devices effectively throughout and within a written text.

- Demonstrate proficient use of college-level, standard written English (e.g., varied word choice, syntax, language conventions, semantics).

- Provide a concluding statement or section that follows from, or supports, the argument or information presented.

- Use a variety of sentence patterns effectively.

- Maintain consistent point of view.

- Apply the conventions of standard English (e.g., avoid inappropriate use of slang, jargon, clichés).

DIRECTIONS: Two topics are presented below. Select one of the topics as the basis for your essay. Read the topics very carefully to make sure you know what you are being asked to do.

> ## Topic 1.
>
> Many Americans disagree on whether children of illegal immigrants should receive a free public education. Evaluate whether this population of children should be provided the same free education as citizens.

> ## Topic 2.
>
> Many employers have expressed concern that college graduates entering the work force often lack soft skills, such as effective communication, interpersonal interactions, time management, and willingness to work on a team. Analyze how these skills are essential for success in the workplace.

Read the two topics again, and select one topic for your essay. In order for your essay to be scored, it must be on only one of these topics, and it must address the entire topic.

In your essay, you should introduce the subject.

Next, you should select one of these two approaches:

* Explain the subject you have chosen.

   OR

* Take a position about your subject and support that position.

At least two evaluators will read your essay to assign a score. They will pay special attention to whether you accomplish the following:

* Determine the purpose of writing to task and audience.

* Provide a section that effectively introduces the topic.

* Formulate a relevant thesis or claim.

* Organize ideas and details effectively.

* Provide adequate, relevant support by citing ample textual evidence. Your response may also include anecdotal experience for added support.

* Use of a variety of transitional devices effectively and demonstrate proficient use of college-level, standard written English (e.g., varied word choice, syntax, language conventions, semantics).

* Provide a concluding statement or section that supports the argument or information presented.

* Use a variety of sentence patterns effectively.

* Maintain consistent point of view.

* Apply the conventions of standard English (that is, avoid inappropriate use of slang, jargon, and clichés).

SCORE of 6

- The essay has a clearly established main idea that the writer fully develops with specific details and examples. Organization is notably logical and coherent. Point of view is consistent. Vocabulary and sentence structure are varied and effective. Errors in sentence structure, usage, and mechanics are few and insignificant.

SCORE of 5

- The essay has a clearly established main idea that is adequately developed and recognizable through specific details and/or examples. Organization follows a logical and coherent pattern. Point of view is mostly consistent. Vocabulary and sentence structure are mostly varied and effective. Occasional errors in sentence structure, usage and mechanics do not interfere with the writer's ability to communicate.

SCORE of 4

- The essay has an adequately stated main idea that is developed with some specific details and examples. Supporting ideas are presented in a mostly logical and coherent manner. Point of view is somewhat consistent. Vocabulary and sentence structure are somewhat varied and effective. Occasional errors in sentence structure, usage, and mechanics may interfere with the writer's ability to communicate.

SCORE of 3

- The essay states a main idea that is developed with generalizations or lists. The essay may contain occasional lapses in logic and coherence, and organization is mechanical. Point of view is ambiguous. Vocabulary and sentence structure are repetitious and often ineffective. A variety of errors in sentence structure, usage, and mechanics sometimes interfere with the writer's ability to communicate.

You will have 50 minutes to draft your multi-paragraph essay. While the rubric does not specify the number of paragraphs, it is a good idea to (1) introduce your topic with a strong thesis, (2) develop body paragraphs that expand upon your topic with concrete supporting details/reasons and relevant examples, and (3) tie the ideas together with an insightful conclusion.

Here are some strategies to help you through the essay portion of the GKT:

1. ***Map out a timing strategy in advance.*** Avoid surprises on test day by mapping out your plan of attack beforehand. Here is our suggestion:

   * 5 minutes to brainstorm ideas and plan

   * 40 minutes to draft your essay

   * 5 minutes to proofread and correct your mistakes

2. ***Read the directions and both topics carefully before choosing one of the topics.*** Do not spend too much time deliberating about your choice. Go with the topic that you relate to and that you can support fully through evidence and examples.

3. ***Brainstorm ideas.*** List everything that comes to your mind about the topic. Circle 3–5 of the strongest supporting ideas. Quickly analyze those ideas and decide which idea fit together best. These supporting ideas will drive your body paragraphs. You should also be able to see your thesis develop from these ideas. Remember, there is no hard-and-fast rule about the number of paragraphs but adding in weak ideas to squeak out an extra paragraph is never advised. If you are comfortable with the tried-and-true five-paragraph essay, stick with three ideas (three body paragraphs). If you think four of your ideas are strong, use them all! Just be mindful of your time. *Cautionary note: If you can't adequately support an idea with relevant details and examples, do not include it!*

4. ***Formulate a thesis statement.*** Do not underestimate the power of the thesis sentence (or sometimes two). This statement guides your entire paper and makes your focus crystal clear to your reader. You need a strong point of view or claim. Avoid simply restating a fact or asking a question. That way, the reader will not have to guess. Please do not say that you are going to say it. Just say it!

5. ***Create a quick mini-outline.*** No Roman numerals needed! This is just a bare bones organizational sketch. You already have your thesis statement and your best supporting ideas ready to go. Putting them in order will help you keep your focus as you write. Here is what it might look like:

Thesis statement: *Children in impoverished areas need to have access to the same quality education programs as children in wealthy areas.*

   * **First supporting idea (Paragraph 2)**: *A quality education is vital for unlocking the potential of any child; socioeconomic status should not be a deciding factor.*

     - Example 1: *St. Louis*

     - Example 2: *Chicago*

   * **Second supporting idea (Paragraph 3)**: *A high-standard education is essential to break the cycle of poverty.*

     - Example 1: *Shaquille O'Neal*

     - Example 2: *Shahid Kahn*

- **Third supporting idea (Paragraph 4):** *Unequal opportunity perpetrates class and racial tension.*
  - Example 1: *Integration issues (busing, discrimination)*
  - Example 2: *Failure to address consequences of poverty in education*

Notice that the thesis and body paragraph supporting idea statements are written in full sentences, but the examples are just quick bullets. Be sure to explain each supporting idea and elaborate on the examples as you write.

6. **Start writing.** You do not have time to second-guess yourself. You can make changes to your original plan as you go if needed.

   - **Introduction.** Brevity is key for your introductory paragraph. It only needs to be a few sentences and should include your thesis. If you get stuck, write your intro last. Simply skip a few (3–5) lines from the top of the answer sheet, and then write your thesis statement on the following line. You can go back after your write your body paragraphs. Getting stumped on how to start is a huge hurdle many writers face on timed tasks. Sometimes, ideas for introductory sentences become clear as you write the body paragraphs.

   - **Body paragraphs.** These paragraphs will make up the bulk of your essay. Elaboration of supporting details and examples is non-negotiable. ***Back up what you say with relevant evidence and examples.*** A good body paragraph will have a supporting idea/claim, explanation of that idea/claim, examples (notice the plural) that are introduced with a transitional phrase such as *for example or for instance*, commentary about the example, and a sentence that paves the way for the next idea. Just as there is no required number of paragraphs, body paragraphs do not need to be a certain number of sentences, but they do need to be fully developed.

   - **Transitional devices.** Use a variety of transitional words, phrases, and sentences to elevate your writing. The basic *first, in addition, finally* are better than nothing; however, using internal transitions and transitional sentences at the end of your body paragraphs will create a clear and logical progression of ideas and give your essay cohesiveness.

   - **Vocabulary.** A big trap that many writers fall into is trying to impress the reader with complicated vocabulary. However, this often backfires. Unless you are 100% positive you know how to use and spell the word, find a synonym you are accustomed to using. In addition, too many lengthy or obscure words actually detract from your point by making your essay tedious to read. Make sure you avoid repeating the same word throughout the entire essay. Again, synonyms are your friends!

   - **Conclusion.** Forget what you learned in elementary and secondary school; restating your thesis and summarizing your ideas does not impress the GKT scorers. They want to see a brief paragraph that ties all your thoughts together with insightful commentary about the topic. This is not the place to introduce any new ideas or ask rhetorical questions. Sometimes suggesting a solution or a call to action is best.

7. **Don't forget to proof!** In timed writing situations, it is tempting to write until time is called. However, to earn a passing score, the essay must be free of errors that interfere with each reader's understanding. In other words, you can have *some* errors in sentence structure, usage, and conventions, but those minor errors should not confuse your readers. In the heat of the moment, you will inadvertently make some mistakes. Correcting these mistakes can be the difference between passing or not passing, so allow at least 5 minutes to proof and correct.

The GKT essay is easy once you understand this writing formula and, of course, practice. You will be given two prompts to choose from. Pick the one that you can write to the easiest. Use the following technique.

1. *Take a position.*

   It is easier to write when you pick one position over another. Most of us are in the middle on many issues; however, when writing an essay in a timed setting, you are better off picking one side or the other.

2. *Map a plan.*

   Use the dry erase board the test center provides to map your essay. This will help you stay organized and concise. Do not spend a ton of time on mapping; just get something down that you can follow as you type the essay.

3. *Keep it organized.*

   Organization is KEY when trying to gain points on the essay. Readers—the people grading your essay—do not want to go around the world to figure out what you are talking about.

   This is how your GKT essay should be organized:

Introduction

This is your first paragraph. In this paragraph, you reword the prompt you are writing to. Change what the prompt says into your own words. You can probably get three sentences out of the prompt. Your thesis statement should be the last sentence of your first paragraph. The thesis statement tells the reader what the essay is going to be about. Everything you write about in this essay must support the thesis statement. The thesis statement should include two distinct ideas or details that you will address in the body of your essay.

Detail Paragraph 1

This is where you discuss the first idea or detail you outlined in your thesis statement. This paragraph should be four to five sentences long. The ONLY thing you should address in this paragraph is ONE of the two details you outlined in your thesis statement. Do not include any other major concepts in this paragraph.

Examples: Be sure to use specific examples that support the detail paragraph. Use anecdotes to support your position and the ideas in this paragraph. Another tip is to use a fake statistic. For example, "In a recent study, 85% of students…" It doesn't matter that the stat is not real. You are fulfilling a writing task; no one is going to check your fake statistic.

Detail Paragraph 2

This is where you discuss the second idea or detail you outlined in your thesis statement. This paragraph should be four to five sentences long. The ONLY thing you should address in this paragraph is the SECOND details you outlined in your thesis statement. Do not include any other major concepts in this paragraph.

Examples: Be sure to use specific examples that support the detail paragraph. Use anecdotes to support your position and the ideas in this paragraph. Another tip is to use a fake statistic. For example, "In a recent study, 85% of students…" It doesn't matter that the stat is not real. You are fulfilling a writing task; no one is going to check your fake statistic.

Conclusion

Wrap it up. This can be difficult, so offer a solution or a call to action. This paragraph should be around three sentences long.

Let's put it together! On the next page is a breakdown of two GKT writing prompts.

Prompt #1: Many Americans disagree on whether children of noncitizens should receive a free, public education. Evaluate whether this population of children should be provided the same free education as citizens are provided.

Intro: Many Americans disagree on public education policy when it comes to noncitizens. Some believe the U.S. should provide an education to all children, while others believe the cost and burden is just too much. All students, no matter what their citizenship, should receive a free public education because this **reduces crime** and **makes our society stronger**.

Detail Paragraph 1: Reduces Crime

In this paragraph, only discuss reducing crime:

- When students are in school, they are off the streets.

- When students are in school, they are working toward an education and thus staying out of trouble.

- In a recent study, 85% of students who were not enrolled in school had committed a crime. (Yes, this is a fake statistic, but it works!)

- Children are susceptible to gang activity when not enrolled in school.

Detail Paragraph 2: Makes Our Society Stronger

In this paragraph, only discuss making society stronger:

- Educated children become part of the community.

- They are involved with school activities and functions (sports, clubs, community service).

- In a recent study, 75% of students who were enrolled in school participated in community service. (Yes, this is a fake statistic, but it works!)

Conclusion: Restate the intro. Quickly restate your position.

Call to action: Everyone should protect our children by allowing all students to attend school, regardless of citizenship.

Prompt #2: As technology plays a bigger and bigger role in education than in the past, teachers are faced with making decisions regarding devices in the classroom. Some teachers use eBooks, YouTube, virtual labs, and more. However, teachers also have to weigh the disadvantages of using new technologies. Evaluate the advantages and disadvantages of using technology in the classroom.

Advantage and disadvantage prompts are the EASIEST because the first detail paragraph can be all about the advantages and the second detail paragraph can be all about the disadvantage. For example:

Introduction: Technology has become an asset in the classroom. Teachers now have access to digital resources like never before. Technology can also create challenges for teachers and students. Before choosing technology for their classrooms, teachers must evaluate the advantages and disadvantages of technology.

Detail Paragraph 1: Advantages

In this paragraph, only discuss advantages:

- Makes life easier.

- eBooks can store many books in one device.

- Students can watch virtual tours of ancient cities.

- In a recent study, students who used technology were 75% more likely to score proficient on their reading tests than those who did not use technology.

Detail Paragraph 1: Disadvantages

In this paragraph, only discuss disadvantages:

- Students can become distracted by technology.

- Students can become addicted to technology.

- Teachers have to compete with the latest technology when they should be teaching.

- Online bullying could be a factor.

- In a recent study, 45% of students said they have been bullied online.

Conclusion: A good way to close an advantage vs. disadvantage prompt is to offer a solution or a balance between the two.

Practice, Practice, Practice! There is no silver bullet. If you want to get better, you have to read more, and you have to write more.

Florida Teacher Certification Exam — General Knowledge Test Essay Guide

This handout is designed to serve as a reference guide for the FTCE GKT Essay.

GKT ESSAY COMPETENCIES AND SKILLS

The essay is evaluated on the writer's ability to demostrate the following capabilities and skills:

- Determine the purpose of writing to task and audience.
- Provide a section that effectively introduces the topic.
- Formulate a relevant thesis or claim.
- Organize ideas and details effectively.
- Provide adequate, relevant support by citing ample textual evidence; response may also include anecdotal experience for added support.
- Use of a variety of transitional devices effectively throughout and within a written text.

- Demonstrate proficient use of college-level, standard written English (e.g., varied word choice, syntax, language conventions, semantics).
- Provide a concluding statement or section that follows from, or supports, the argument or information presented.
- Use a variety of sentence patterns effectively.
- Maintain consistent point of view.
- Apply the conventions of standard English (e.g., avoid inappropriate use of slang, jargon, clichés).

ESSAY FORMULA

Step 1: Thesis Statement. Choose topic and type the prompt on the computer in the space provided.

Step 2: Develop Outline. Use the dry erase board to map out the essay.

Detail paragraph 1 (benefits/item 1)	Detail paragraph 2 (challenges/item 2)

1. Supporting idea
   • Tangible example
   • Tangible example
2. Supporting idea
   • Tangible example
   • Tangible example
3. Supporting idea
   • Tangible example
   • Tangible example
	1. Supporting idea
	   • Tangible example
	   • Tangible example
	2. Supporting idea
	   • Tangible example
	   • Tangible example
	3. Supporting idea
	   • Tangible example
	   • Tangible example

Step 3: Write Essay— Use outline to type essay. Use thesis for introduction and conclusion. Include a call to action sentence.

Step 4: Proof Read—Read back through the essay carefully for spelling and grammatical errors.

SAMPLE ESSAY MAP

Step 1: Thesis Statement. Research conducted by the U.S. Department of Labor shows a demand for teachers in math, English language arts, and science. Explain why there is such a demand.

Detail paragraph 1 (teacher shortage)	Detail paragraph 2 (increased need)

1. Burn out
   • More responsibilities for teachers/level of effort
   • Rigorous schedules and accountability measures
2. Lack of support
   • Low salaries for teachers
   • Lack of classroom resources (technology, filed trips, aides)
3. Certification exams
   • Additional test requirements for subject area teachers
   • High costs for teachers to take and retake exams
	1. Workforce
	   • Employers want more math, science, English language arts
	   • College program requirements to prepare students
	2. National initiatives in math, science and English
	   • Private sector push for STEM programs
	   • More students want science, math and English classes
	3. Student support
	   • Students struggle, requiring more teachers
	   • Students striving for subject area scholarships to get ahead

Step 3: Write Essay. Call to action— Policy makers need to provide adequate support to education to match the increased demand for teachers in math, science, and English language arts.

Step 4: Proof Read.

Florida Teacher Certification Exam — General Knowledge Test Essay Guide
TIPS AND COMMON ERRORS

TIME MANAGEMENT	
Step 1: Thesis Statement	1-2 minutes
Step 2: Develop Outline	15-20 minutes
Step 3: Write Essay	15-20 minutes
Step 4: Proofread	5 minutes

AFFECT VS EFFECT	
Affect (usually a verb)	**Effect (usually a noun)**
• They were negatively affected.	• The negative effect of testing.
• Students are affected by the test.	• Create a calming effect.
• Funding affects the schedule.	• The effect is positive.

PASSIVE VOICE VS ACTIVE VOICE

Passive Voice (Incorrect)	Active Voice (Correct)
• More research should be conducted.	• Lawmakers should conduct more research.
• Student achievement will be assessed.	• Teachers will assess student achievement.
• The test will be taken by students on Monday.	• Students will take the test on Monday.
• This room will be cleaned today.	• Pam and Jim will clean this room today.
• Research was conducted by the university.	• The university conducted research.

FEWER VS LESS

Fewer (things that can be counted)	Less (things that cannot be counted)
I have fewer dollars than before.	I have less money than before.
There are fewer teachers than in previous years.	There is less funding for education than other institutions.
She scored fewer points on the first test than on the second.	He has less hair than before he had kids.

CLICHÉS

Avoid using trite expressions and cliché terms in the essay. The table below provides a list of commonly used clichés.

• State-of-the-art	• A diamond in the rough	• Eleventh hour
• In today's world	• The calm before the storm	• Force of nature
• Nowadays	• Mutually exclusive	• Have high hopes
• Only time will tell	• Silver lining	• It's a small world
• Read between the lines	• Back to square one	• Light at the end of the tunnel
• Just a matter of time	• Big fish in a small pond	• On the spot
• A clean slate	• Day in, day out	• Seize the day

TRANSITIONS
Use transitional expressions to connect ideas.

- Time: first, next, also, finally, meanwhile, recently, again
- Related: again, also, then, equally, likewise, furthermore
- Difference: besides, contrary, instead, regardless
- Comparison: although, nevertheless, despite that, however
- Importance: certainly, indeed, in fact, definitely
- Example: for example, specifically, for instance, such as
- Conclusion: altogether, in summary, finally, to summarize

PROOFREADING CHECKLIST
Leave enough time to review the essay for common errors.

- Check spelling
- That versus who
- Their, there, and they're
- Commas and punctuation
- Less than, more than
- Review for structure and organization
- Avoid using first and second person (I, we, my, you, your)

53991987R00105

Made in the
USA
Lexington, KY